Living the Spirit-filled Life

Living the Spirit-filled Life

DOUGLAS COOPER

Pacific Press Publishing Association
Boise, Idaho
Montemorelos, Nuevo Leon, Mexico
Oshawa, Ontario, Canada

Cover by Tim Larson

Copyright © 1985 by
Pacific Press Publishing Association
Printed in United States of America
All Rights Reserved

ISBN 0-8163-0595-1

*If we live in the Spirit,
let us also
walk in the Spirit*—Galatians 5:25

Contents

Games Christians Play	9
Poor Man, Rich Man	18
You Can Make It Happen!	25
The Breath of Life	37
Welcome to the Ministry	47
The Crucible of Love	63
Take Your Love to Town	77

Games Christians Play

Ye do always resist the Holy Ghost: as your fathers did, so do ye. Acts 7:51.

Several years ago psychiatrist Eric Berne wrote a fascinating book titled *Games People Play*. With tongue-in-cheek, he described certain delightful diversions people seem to enjoy—such "games" as "I'll try to help you"—(providing you don't get better!) or "I'll look for work"—(providing I don't have to find a job!).

"Patients often play a game with therapists called 'help me, but don't cure me', " Berne says. "Often what they mean is 'I don't really want to be cured but I will let you make me a better neurotic!' "[1]

It would be great fun to write a book called *Games Christians Play*, describing such games as "Jesus doesn't love you when you hit the kitty cat," which mommies could play with their three-year-olds!

This book could recommend that churchgoers play "courtroom." (If you were arrested for being a Christian, would there be enough evidence to convict you?)

It could describe people who play a game with God called "You can save me"—(as long as You don't change me!).

It could detail a game some Christians play with the devil called "spiritual darebase"—(see how close you can come to temptation without actually sinning!).

Such a book could even carry a large appendix containing helpful hints for Christians ("Twenty-three surefire excuses for skipping prayer meeting," or "Thirty-nine ways to witness without leaving your easy chair!).

The book would not be complete unless it included one of the oldest religious games of all—the "secret salvation" game. A few Christians still play it. The idea of this one is to see if you can go a lifetime without telling anyone that you have salvation. Under the rules it is quite all right to say, "I *hope* I will be saved someday," or "I am working hard to get rid of enough bad habits so I can be saved."

The main point of this game is never to confess to anyone that you have eternal life right now. You may sing "Redeemed, How I Love to Proclaim It!"—but you dare not *say* so.

Another very popular game in Christendom today is called "baby with the bathwater." This one is similar to the previous game. The difference is that here you must *never* EVER say that you are "baptized with the Holy Spirit." If you do, you must go immediately to Fanatics' Fringe or Charismatics' Corner!

A master gamesman invented this one, and it has been easy for him to find players. No one wants to be branded a religious fanatic. The idea of this game is to keep people away from a genuine spiritual experience by inventing an undesirable counterfeit. Thus the baby gets thrown out with the bathwater, and nobody wins. Except the fiend who made up the game! This is a great tragedy, for after the cross, the doctrine of the Holy Spirit is the most important yet most neglected doctrine in all Christianity.

One author—who studied in detail what Christ spoke about to determine His favorite topic—once wrote, "Christ, the Great Teacher, had an infinite variety of subjects from which to choose, but the one upon which He dwelt most largely was the endowment of the Holy Spirit. What great things He predicted for the church because of this endowment. Yet what subject is less dwelt upon now? What promise is less fulfilled?"[2]

For all too many Christians, the same lamentable uncertainity that steals away their assurance of salvation also shadows their appropriation of the Holy Spirit by faith. They sing with great fervor, "Baptize us anew with power from on high." Yet if you ask the average Christian today whether he is baptized with the Spirit, he will look surprised and say, "Why, of course not—I am not a charismatic!" Or perhaps he will say, "Well, I hope to be someday," or "I am working on getting my life together so that I can be sometime."

As surely as Christ made eternal life possible by His death on the cross, He also made the Spirit-filled life possible for the Christian right now. To deny these great gifts from the throne room of heaven is to be deprived of both peace and power.

Believers may feel that it is a great insult when some choose to reject Christ's atonement. Yet they may be grieving His great heart of love fully as much by ignoring—or rejecting by default—the filling of the Holy Spirit.

The great evangelist Charles Finney once said, "Christians are as guilty for not being filled with the Spirit as sinners are for not repenting."

The work of the Holy Spirit includes far more than many Christians realize. To bring us to and through the new birth is one part of His work—as Jesus made plain to Nicodemus. And this mighty miracle of the Spirit's power is recognized by a baptism—the baptism "with water" of which John the Baptist spoke.[3]

But it is sadly possible for a Christian to experience personally the Spirit's power in being born again and yet never experience *the rest* of what the Spirit is ready to do in his life. For the Holy Spirit is available to do far more for us than to see us through the new birth. This is only a part of

His work. How appalling that so many of us either don't know or don't care that He is also available to fill us with supernatural power to witness and to overcome sin!

This mighty infilling of the Spirit is also marked by a baptism—the baptism "with fire" which John the Baptist said Jesus would make possible.

Undoubtedly it is God's intent that as soon as we have been born again through the Spirit's power, we begin immediately to experience also the fullness of His power to help us witness and to grow. For both physically and spiritually, birth *must* be followed by growth.

Yet, tragically, many Christians—possibly through misunderstanding or ignorance—are like the believers Paul encountered in Ephesus.

These men had been baptized with water, but to Paul's question, "Did you receive the Holy Spirit when you believed?" they responded, "We have never even heard that there is a Holy Spirit."[4]

Like a destitute farmer, unaware that under his fields lies a fortune in gold, they had been living far beneath their privileges. But that was now to change, for "when Paul had laid his hands upon them, the Holy Spirit came on them."[5]

Jesus Christ did not die only that men might have forgiveness of sin. He also sacrificed Himself that men might begin sharing immediately in His very nature and sonship. He did not die only that men might be born again, but that they might also go on from there to really *live* again—to experience an unprecedented power to live God's love in the world.

The Saviour did not die that believers might be legally pardoned—only to be put on ice until He could return someday to restore His image in them. He died that every Christian might be ignited by the Holy Spirit and begin at once—through this transforming, supernatural Presence—to take on the characteristics of divinity! He died that men and women might share in His sacred task of revealing God's love to the world. He died that you and I might begin to share in His divine nature right now!

The significance of Christ's sacrifice is indicated in Isaiah 53:12. When taken literally from the Hebrew, the first phrase reads, "therefore will I divide his portion with the many." The priesthood and sonship of Jesus is the sacred heritage He has given to be shared among His followers. This He did to equip them to take His place—to be His representatives in this world.

No vain philosophy, no dry intellectual theory, no milk-toast, pie-in-the-sky, namby-pamby, don't-upset-the-apple-cart system for nominal believers—this thing called Christianity. Instead, it is a far more radical and revolutionary force than even most modern believers imagine. The religion of Jesus Christ is nothing less than an omnipotent, transforming power.

That radical element in Christianity which once aroused the world's hatred toward believers seems no longer to be present in the church. This would strongly suggest that the baptism by fire is being virtually ignored today. No longer is it especially unpopular or dangerous or costly to be a Christian. And that is a very great shame.

The Christians in the early church were no particular threat to the powers of evil—until the day of Pentecost. Then every devil in hell began to tremble at the thought of dealing with the weakest of the saints. Talk about "power to the people!"

If only Christ's disciples today could see themselves as God sees them! If only they could live up to their true spiritual potential! If only they could rise to their privileges!

An old Indian story tells of a brave who discovered an eagle's egg. He placed it in the nest of one of the village chickens. The eaglet hatched with the brood and grew up with them. In time he learned to scratch busily in the dirt for seeds and bugs. He learned to pull worms from the ground and to cluck and cackle. Like his fellows, he was easily alarmed by any imagined threat. He flew only with a brief, awkward thrashing of wings and flurry of feathers—and then only a few feet above the ground. After all, that is how chickens are supposed to fly.

Years passed, and the bird grew old. But one day he chanced to look up from his continual scratching in the dirt and saw a most magnificent creature floating effortlessly above him in the cloudless sky. Riding with graceful majesty on the powerful wind currents, it soared above the high mountain ridges with hardly a beat of its strong, golden wings.

"What a beautiful bird!" he remarked to one of his neighbors. "What is it?"

"That's an eagle—the king of birds," the chicken clucked. "But don't give it a second thought. You could never be like him."

So the eagle put it all out of his mind and went on scratching away in the dirt. He died one day, still thinking he was a chicken.[6]

God has promised believers that they may "mount up with wings as eagles."[7] Every spirit-filled Christian may lead an exciting life of excellence, splendor, and promise. How sad that so many believers scratch around the chicken coop when they could be riding the mountain crests!

Any religion that does not lift people up—that does not make them into something more than they ever dreamed they could be—is a counterfeit. A Christianity that focuses only on clearing up a legal sin problem, offering the believer nothing more until the second coming—a Christianity concerned primarily with correct belief and accurate theology—is a system having the form of godliness but denying the power of it.

This transforming power that makes genuine Christianity

such a revolutionary force has as its source the baptism so often ignored—the baptism with fire. "Ye shall receive power, after that the Holy Ghost is come upon you."[8]

To take full advantage of all that God offers, one needs to experience both water baptism and fire baptism. If conversion is being made into a new creature with the legal right to fly, becoming Spirit-filled is the flying! It is no accident that a bird—a dove—is the symbol of the Holy Spirit in the Bible.

Jesus was understandably anxious to return to heaven when His work was finished here on earth. But some are puzzled as to why He only ministered here for three and a half years. "Why did He go back to heaven so quickly?" they ask. "Why didn't He at least stay until He was fifty or sixty years old and do more preaching and healing?"

Actually, it is remarkable that the Saviour stayed here as long as He did. He would doubtless have preferred to finish His work in three and a half *months*. True, He did not want to leave His followers behind, but He was very anxious to return to His Father quickly *so that He could send the Holy Spirit to begin a whole new powerful ministry to His people*.

"Nevertheless I tell you the truth; it is expedient for you that I go away: for if I go not away, the Comforter will not come unto you; but if I depart, I will send him unto you."[9]

The dictionary says the word *expedient* means "conducive to an advantage." And what a marvelous advantage the coming of the Comforter has been to every believer since!

Jesus had come to reveal to the world the truth about God. His mission was to reveal the breadth and intensity of God's love in startling and remarkable ways. Yet in His humanity He was limited to being in one place at a time. His eagerness to return to heaven was prompted by the knowledge that His sacrifice on the cross had opened the way for a very great miracle. Now *any* believer could have the Holy Spirit living in him—just as the Spirit had dwelt in the Saviour!

The way was clear for something to take place that Christ cared about passionately. Now God's love and character could be lived out, not just through one solitary life, but through hundreds, thousands, millions of lives!

Each Christian could now take up Christ's own high and holy mission. Each believer could begin—through the indwelling of the Spirit symbolized by the baptism with fire—to partake of the divine nature as Christ had. This would bring the truth about God and His love before the entire waiting world.

Ultimate privilege! Humanity could now become the very home of divinity! "In whom ye also are builded together *for an habitation of God* through the Spirit."[10]

Christ certainly existed before He took on human form as a babe in the manger. He created, He loved, He ministered as the divine Son of God. Yet something very special happened when He was born into a human body. He began a very personal, very special, very powerful ministry to the world at that time which could not have been accomplished any other way. Being able to work in a human frame made the difference.

The Holy Spirit too has existed from time immemorial. He has played an active part in ministering to the world. But just as Jesus was born into a human body, so the Holy Spirit needed to become incarnate to carry out His new and special ministry in the world. But whereas Christ reached out to the world from within just one human body, the Holy Spirit would now reach out through many! The Holy Spirit was incarnated at Pentecost. Some of the best and most exciting good news of Christianity is that the Spirit now lives in every believer who chooses the baptism with fire—who chooses to be filled with Him! "What? know ye not that *your body* is the temple of the Holy Ghost *which is in you,* which ye have of God, and ye are not your own?"[11]

The day of Pentecost was the dawn of a new age for the

follower of God. Never before had such a privilege been extended or such dynamic power been offered. Christians today should celebrate Pentecost with at least as much fervor as they do Christmas. A whole new arsenal of spiritual weapons was then placed at their disposal. What they received that day was a down payment on the heavenly inheritance, allowing heaven to begin here and now for every believer. "That Holy Spirit of promise, which is the earnest [the down payment] of our inheritance until the redemption of the purchased possession, unto the praise of his glory."[12] The year A.D. 33 was a very good year!

As shocking as it may seem, Christ's death alone—to earn men a legal pardon from the wages of sin—would not have been adequate to accomplish all of God's purposes for the world. If Jesus had gone to the cross, but the Holy Spirit had not come to personally apply its benefits to the lives of Christ's followers, *the cross would have been in vain*. "The Spirit is given as a regenerating agency, to make effectual the salvation wrought by the death of our Redeemer."[13]

The Spirit was given to apply the benefits of the cross to every believer's life. The Holy Spirit does not provide forgiveness of sin. Jesus did that at Calvary. But the Spirit provides power—power to live God's love before the world and to break through the strongest barriers men and women may erect to keep God out!

The baptism of the Spirit makes Christ's death worth the cost, for it restores to man the purpose of his creation—oneness with God, personal fellowship with the Almighty.

Therefore if one does not receive the baptism with fire—if he does not actively claim the filling of the Spirit by faith—he ignores the very blood that won for him the highest and best gift Heaven could bestow.

With what joy, then, should we contemplate the privilege of providing God the Spirit a flesh-and-blood expression—an incarnation in our time.

Poor Man, Rich Man

I know thy works, and tribulation, and poverty, (but thou art rich). Revelation 2:9.

When the newspaper carried the account, many people who knew who she was were shocked. They had watched her for years—this little "bag lady." No one could remember when she hadn't been around the neighborhood. A dumpy little character with frizzy gray hair, she was easily identifiable by her tattered coat and her habit of walking the back alleys to scrounge the best of the pickings from the garbage cans. She lived in poverty in a ramshackle little cottage, the yard overgrown with weeds.

According to the paper, the cause of her death was starvation. It was surmised that she had become ill, been unable to make her usual rounds of the alleys to get scraps to eat, and eventually just wasted away. When the police came to investigate, they made a most incredible discovery. After wading through stacks of trash, empty cans, thirty-year-old magazines, and bundles of rags, they found—hidden in little cubbyholes, under flower pots, in old vases, and under her mattress—a hoard of gold and silver coins and bullion. They found paper money too. Greenbacks. Hundreds of thousands of dollars of them. And stock certificates and savings account passbooks.

All in all the total came to slightly over three million dollars. The little bag lady who starved herself to death had been one of the wealthiest women in the city. Years before, she had received a large inheritance from a rich father and had never used any of it.

Every Christian is a spiritual billionaire. A vast wealth of spiritual treasure was credited to every believer's account the day Christ died. Another giant deposit was made on the day of Pentecost.

How utterly tragic that so many are starving in spiritual poverty while Heaven's richest gifts go unclaimed. By many, these gifts are seldom appropriated, seldom appreciated. People who have been invited to a daily spiritual banquet attempt to survive on scraps.

Not only does the believer thus deprive himself—he also has no resources to share with others. One cannot give away something he does not have. The very essence of Christianity is sharing with others the wonderful things one receives from God. To fail to draw fully upon the marvelous spiritual heritage provided by the sacrifice of the Son of God—and to fail to share these desperately needed riches with a dying world—is to fail in fulfilling the very purpose for our creation and existence.

If believers would only begin to wake up and realize who they are and what they have! They are children of the King! They are a royal priesthood! A chosen generation! "We are the children of God: and if children, then heirs; heirs of God, and joint-heirs with Christ."[1]

If believers are indeed joint-heirs with Christ, there must be something very special that God gave to His Son that He has also provided for every Christian. What then is this great spiritual asset which Jesus had and which may also be joyfully claimed by every follower of God? Is it His immortality? No, for divinity alone is immortal. Is it His perfection? No, for no Christian can ever possess the absolute perfection of Christ.

Christ's divinity, immortality, and perfection were uniquely His and were not shared with others when He came to this world. Indeed, the exercise of His own divinity He voluntarily laid aside. His perfection, while essential to His being the Saviour, was not what empowered Him to be the Saviour.

Christ lived a perfect life for thirty years in the little town of Nazareth—but this alone would not have been enough to save the world. He took loving care of his widowed mother. He made quality baby cribs and dining-table chairs. During this time He seemingly accomplished no great good for humanity. His perfection appeared to achieve little more than to convince His fellow townsmen that He was strange and out of step.

During these years, which represented most of His life on earth, He worked no miracles. He attracted no disciples. He preached no evangelistic sermons. He healed no cripples. He had no public ministry of any kind. And He was no particularly active or apparent threat to the kingdom of evil.

Jesus was not yet prepared or equipped to save the world. He needed an extra measure of power from beyond Himself—a special gift, a special heritage from God.

The years passed—and then it happened. The quiet life of the carpenter from Nazareth was revolutionized and transformed by a tremendous endowment from heaven. "And Jesus himself began to be about thirty years of age." "And the Holy Ghost descended in a bodily shape like a dove upon him."[2]

Until that day most people saw Jesus as just another Galilean craftsman. But when God opened up the treasurehouse of heaven and bestowed His best gift on His Son-in-human-form—the special anointing of the Holy Spirit—Jesus could then become all He was meant to be and do all that He was meant to do.

This special bestowal of the Holy Spirit is also God's best gift to the Christian. It is, in fact, the highest good, the greatest spiritual treasure, that heaven can bestow on humanity. The reception of this gift is one of the primary means by which believers become joint heirs with Christ. And this gift is what makes the Christian all he was meant to be and empowers him to do all he was meant to do.

"God anointed Jesus of Nazareth with the Holy Ghost and with power: who went about doing good, and healing all that were oppressed of the devil."[3]

Now the Nazarene was empowered for a ministry to the whole world. He was no longer just Jesus the carpenter. He was Jesus the Christ! Now every devil in hell trembled at His name!

Jesus had, of course, known the indwelling of the Spirit from His birth. The Spirit had been His constant, mighty source of power to live a sinless life. How else could Jesus have done it?

But on the banks of the Jordan the Holy Spirit descended to anoint Him with a new and supernatural power. Now Jesus could show the entire universe—through electrifying deeds and words—what God is really like. He now had power to transform the most determined rebels into loyal sons and daughters of His Father.

Before His own personal Pentecost, Jesus was—as the name Jesus indicates—the world's Saviour. But when the Dove descended upon Him, He became also Christ—the Anointed One.

A revolutionary change took place in Christ's ministry when He received this special gift from heaven. "And Jesus returned in the power of the Spirit into Galilee."[4] He went into the little village synagogue He had attended faithfully since childhood. Now His fellow Nazarenes saw Him as they never had before. A drastic change was seen in their friend, the gentle carpenter! "The Spirit of the Lord is upon me," He told them, "because he hath anointed me to preach the gospel to the poor; he hath sent me to heal the brokenhearted, to preach deliverance to the captives, and recovering of sight to the blind, to set at liberty them that are bruised, to preach the acceptable year of the Lord."[5]

Jesus was possessed of a whole new vision. No longer was His focus on making the best-finished cabinets in a little Galilean village. Now He burned with a soul-passion to finish God's work in the whole world! Those who had heard the formerly quiet craftsman were now "astonished at his doctrine: for his word was with power."[6]

Unquestionably, Jesus had received a marvelous inheritance from heaven when the Holy Spirit descended upon Him. This was part of His divine birthright as the Son of God. Some may say, "This is true, but that was a special gift just for Christ. We certainly don't deserve such a gift for ourselves. We aren't entitled to it."

Incredible as it may seem, Christ wishes to share this great treasure from heaven with every one of His followers. He wants each of them to receive it as fully as He did. Because He knew that His followers could draw on this divine resource, He could make an absolutely astonishing statement: "He that believeth on me, the works that I do shall he do also; and greater works than these shall he do; because I go unto my Father."[7] He was eager to return to heaven so that He could send the Spirit to empower His followers.[8]

Never forget that Jesus Christ did not die on the cross only to provide believers with eternal life. He died that sinners could be forgiven and restored to a relationship with God for a *purpose*. That profound purpose was that they might receive His inheritance and take up His task—that they might be equipped and empowered to live out God's love and character and personality as He did! *Starting now!*

Through the indwelling of the Holy Spirit, believers are brought into full sonship with God. And as God's sons and daughters we become joint heirs with Christ. "As many as are led by the Spirit of God, they are the sons of God. . . . Ye have received the Spirit of adoption, whereby we cry,

Abba, Father. The Spirit itself beareth witness with our spirit, that we are the children of God: and if children, then heirs; heirs of God, and joint heirs with Christ."[9]

It was not Christ's sinless life that equipped Him for a ministry to the world—as significant as that was in qualifying Him to be a perfect sacrifice for sin. He lived without sin during His entire life in Nazareth without publicly ministering to the world.

Perhaps too often we seek to find in our good behavior our highest qualification for service. But the example of Christ Himself suggests we might better concentrate on seeking the fullness of the Holy Spirit. Moments of walking in the Spirit can accomplish what years of struggling in the flesh might produce in spiritual maturity and in enlarging our capacity to love and serve.

Flying my airplane over a large city at night is always a great thrill to me. The vast glow of lights below makes it appear one is flying over a galaxy turned upside down.

Over a metropolis such as Los Angeles, the pale white glow of the street lamps below blends with warmer, yellow tones of light from the windows of hundreds of uncounted thousands of homes and apartments. Skyscrapers loom like torches. Accenting it all are flowing streams of white and red light—as automobiles form a moving river of luminescence along the freeways. From horizon to horizon stretches this marvelous display of the power of electricity.

Amazingly, little more than a short century and a half ago, the brightest light to be found in any city was that of a candle. When night came the whole world virtually went dark until the next sunrise.

Yet electricity was not just recently created. It has been a very real and present force on this planet from the beginning. As much electricity was available a thousand years ago as today. But man did not tap its immense potential until just recently!

24 LIVING THE SPIRIT-FILLED LIFE

The Holy Spirit is a dynamic source of spiritual power. It has been fully available to empower believers for their task for almost 2000 years. Yet only a few tap its potent energy. An occasional burst of light and power is seen here or there. Generally, however, believers struggle to function by candlelight, when they could be walking in the brilliance of a thousand suns!

Christians are shocked when modern Jews pointedly state they do not believe in Jesus Christ as Messiah and Saviour. They are saddened by a religion that ignores the marvelous blessing of an ever-present Saviour—a religion that insists on looking only to the future for the fulfillment of all its hopes.

Yet many Christians are guilty of viewing the Holy Spirit in the way the Jewish religion views Jesus! Many believers insist that the baptism of the Spirit is not yet available. "The Holy Spirit will be poured out sometime in the future," they say. But they forget that A.D. 33 was a very good year! They cheat themselves of immense power. They miss out on the incomparable blessing of experiencing a very *present* Holy Spirit dwelling in *their* lives—living in *their* bodies!

Two thousand years ago Jesus Christ gave a promise that stands for all today. "I will pray the Father, and he shall give you another Comforter, *that he may abide with you for ever.*" "If I depart, I will send him unto you."[10]

The Comforter has come! The heavenly fire has fallen! This great treasure from God's storehouse is here for you and me. This is a significant part of the "good news" of the gospel The Holy Spirit is our precious heritage as sons and daughters of God and joint heirs with Jesus.

With what deep joy should we celebrate our treasure!

With what abandoned profligacy should we spend its unending riches on others!

With what eager expectancy should we claim the promised power!

You Can Make It Happen!

Be keener than ever to work out the salvation that God has given you with a proper sense of awe and responsibility. Philippians 2:12, Phillips.

A preacher once purchased a very run-down old ranch. Seeing its lamentable condition, some of his friends thought he had taken leave of his senses in deciding to buy it. He had bought himself a few acres of weeds, some gopher holes and leaking irrigation lines, and a run-down fence a jackrabbit could have knocked over. The barn had more shingles off the roof than on, and the roads were full of potholes.

The parson seemed not to mind. Faithfully he took his days off each week and worked from dawn until dark on the old place. His yearly vacation was devoted to the same cause with equal intensity. He mixed cement, plowed weeds, replaced broken windows, and repaired plumbing. After many months the ranch began to look good again. When the restoration was almost complete and everything was in order, the pastor received a neighborly visit from a farmer who lived down the road.

Farmer Brown took a long look at the revitalized property. He nodded his head in approval and said, "Well, preacher, it looks like you and God really accomplished something here."

The pastor paused, wiped the sweat from his brow, and answered, "It's interesting you should say that, Mr. Brown. You should have seen this place when God had it all to Himself!"[1]

Christians are in this world to act for God. You and I are to be His hands and feet. Our smile is to be His smile—our touch His touch—our love His love.

God provided Jesus with a human body, that Christ might express the Father's love and do the Father's work in this world. Now God wishes to use *our* bodies—with the Holy Spirit living in them—to carry out His purposes and reveal His love and character on earth.

Spirit-filled Christians exist for one grand purpose—*dynamic action!* My favorite book of the Bible is not called the Book of Thoughts. Nor is it titled the Book of Beliefs or the Book of Doctrines. It is called the Book of Acts!

Jesus "went about doing good," the Bible says. How tragic that modern Christianity has largely been reduced to a spectator sport! True religion is like the greyhound or the eagle. It is designed for action!

"Do . . . and you will know," promised Christ.[2] Only in experience and action does Christianity confirm itself in the soul of the believer. God blesses action—not good intentions. He is able to do little through people who merely sit around and think good thoughts and hold right beliefs.

You do not believe Christianity so much as you live it! You do not espouse Christianity so much as you do it!

I have written five books, and I am working on two more. Some people call me a writer. I like the title, but it is a hard one to live up to. Writing is hard work. Someone has said that "writing is easy—you just sit in front of a typewriter until small drops of blood begin to form on your forehead!"

Sometimes I really envy carpenters or mechanics. They come home at the end of the day all dirty and sweaty—with grease under their fingernails—and their wives know they have really been *doing* something.

Do you know how difficult it can be trying to convince your wife that you have been doing something—that you have been working really hard—when you have been sitting in front of a typewriter and looking out a window for two hours?

I have tried to think of a way to be a writer without doing any writing, but so far it escapes me. The time comes when you have to sit down in front of a typewriter and put some words on paper.

I have found that a lot of people would like to be writers like a lot of people would like to be returned missionaries. But you have to be a missionary before you can be a returned missionary and dress up in costumes and give lectures on far-away, exotic places!

You also have to write in order to be a writer. You have to do carpentery in order to be a carpenter. And if you are really a Christian, you will "do" Christianity. You will love if you are truly a Christian—for love is the highest form of Christian action.

Love is, after all, not just something you feel. It is something you do—something you do for the very best good of another person, regardless of how you happen to feel about them.

The time has come for a group of Spirit-filled Christians to start doing their Christianity. What we need is a twentieth-century Book of Acts.

Far too long have we simply *talked* about truth. Now nothing could be more urgent than that we *become* truth. Far too long have we talked and philosophized and written about love. Now we must also *become* love—as Jesus did.

We must put skin on love through the Holy Spirit living in us as He did in Christ.

Can you imagine it? Infinite love—the love and personality and presence of Almighty God—was reduced to the size of a grain of sand! God in DNA and red corpuscles! Love encoded in twenty-three pairs of chromosomes! Infinite love emerging in muscle and blood, skin and bones! Divinity in diapers! Love in swaddling clothes. Love in a homespun white-linen cloth. Love in donkey-hide, made-in-Galilee sandals.

And today? Why not love in coveralls? Love in Nike running shoes and Calvin Klein jeans?

The Holy Spirit has been given to help make spiritual things *happen* in our lives. Salvation—the most basic doctrine of Christianity—must not only be believed intellectually, but it must be allowed to *happen* in the life. Salvation must not only be a doctrine to be believed but an experience to be celebrated. Daily.

Some believers have cheated themselves for years by focusing almost exclusively on intellectual truth—on spiritual head knowledge. *Just because you have the correct belief about something does not mean you have that something itself!* Because you have the doctrine you do not necessarily have the experience. A terrific mistake is made in substituting spiritual logic for spiritual life.

One thing is certain. When it comes to spiritual truth, we will never really know what we do not act upon—what we do not experience. Far too long have Christians been afraid to experience their religion. "Oh, it's dangerous to focus your religion on experience," many say. While it is unwise to base one's Christianity on feelings, it is dangerous *not* to base it on experience. And there is a vast difference between the two.

If you are not experiencing anything in your religion, it is a counterfeit. It is not Christianity. Christianity always has been, is, and always will be a religion marked by experience. Marked by how it changes people's lives—how it moves them not just to believe differently but to *act* very differently. It compels them to do things they would not otherwise do—to say things they would not otherwise say—to be something they would not otherwise be.

Christianity is an experience. It happens to you. It changes you and keeps on changing you. It is more mystical than intellectual, for it is grasped and experienced more with the heart than with the head. *Never limit your spiritual life to that which is comprehensible. Every mystic is not a Christian, but every Christian is a mystic!*

After all, in its best and highest sense, mysticism is the very indwelling of God. That is what Jesus offered every believer when He promised the coming of the Comforter. And that is not something that can be explained logically—it can only be experienced. While the keenest human mind cannot fathom such a miraculous mystery, the humblest saint can experience it within his heart.

"Even the mystery which hath been hid from ages and from generations, but now is made manifest to his saints: to whom God would make known what is the riches of the glory of this mystery among the Gentiles; which is Christ in you, the hope of glory."[3]

Christ miraculously, mysteriously dwelling inside His followers through the Holy Spirit—this too is the gospel. People experiencing their God. God happening in their lives—living in them, loving through them. Can you explain it? No. Can you experience it? Yes. F. D. Huntington has written, "While reason is puzzling itself about mystery, faith is turning it to daily bread and feeding on it thankfully in her heart of hearts."

Christianity, then, is something you do—as well as something you are. It is truth come alive. It is love with skin on it. It is giving joy an expression in eyes and smiles. It is making care real with the touch of a hand on a shoulder or a warm embrace or a gentle word of sympathy.

Believers simply must learn to take some of the responsibility to make spiritual things happen. You cannot accept Christianity intellectually and then just sit back and wait.

Today we hear a lot about "taking charge of your life." Popular psychology has much to say about taking charge of your emotional life, your financial life, or your social life instead of just sitting back and waiting to see what will work out—instead of being at the whim of circumstances or other people.

Christians must take charge of their religious lives. That is what the Bible is talking about when it says to "work out your own salvation." It is telling believers to take responsibility for their own spiritual lives! It is telling them to realize that through the power God makes available, *they can make spiritual things happen!*

Fellow Christians, we are not simply what we think. We are not what we believe. And we are not what we feel. *We are and always will be what we will and what we do!*

Genuine Christian experience is not something to be afraid of—because it is not the product of fickle feelings. It does not consist of logically grasping and believing correct truths. Important as intellectual enlightenment may be, it is not the heart of true religion. Even the devils believe—and tremble. Christians say they believe—but often seem not even to have the sense to tremble! Anyone—devil or human—should tremble who would make of the spiritual life only a belief system. Why? Because to do so is totally to miss the heart of it all.

The center of Christianity is the will. It is the citadel of religion. It is the seat of true Christian experience. Your will is your most Godlike faculty. More than anything else it makes a human being more than a mere super-animal—more than a super-computer. The will is special because it is the will which makes things happen. The will is the ultimate force in the life. To be is to do. It is in the doing of things that our Christianity, our identity, our reality is established. Through the will the believer reveals whether he is indeed a son of God. Has he willed himself to this position? Is he using his Spirit-controlled will to get the things of God done in this world?

The will is much deeper than emotion or reason, for it is

the center of true experience and godly action. We are what we choose to do! Our emotions merely express how we feel. Our intellect is what we think. But with our wills we choose what we do, what we are, and what we will become!

Watchman Nee has written, "Man may experience joy, comfort and peace in believing in God. He may understand His majesty and amass much wonderful knowledge; but does he possess any genuine union with Him if his will is not united with God's?"[4]

"God's delight is in having His people . . . do what He would have them do. . . . All else which is labeled spirituality, such as holy and happy feelings or prize-winning thoughts is but an outward show."[5]

Even such a dynamic, exciting spiritual concept as the baptism of the Holy Spirit is approached, claimed, and experienced, not with intellectual comprehension alone, nor with the emotions, but with the will.

Love itself is not an emotion. Love—the great, beating heart of Christianity—is a state of the will or it is nothing at all. Love is something which—through Christ's indwelling power—you make happen. That's right. You can make love happen. *Love is choosing to do or say what is for the very best good of another person regardless of what you think about him or how you feel toward him.*

In a marital counseling situation it is always tragic to hear a husband say, "Well, I just don't feel anything for her anymore." Many assume that because they do not have the same kind or depth of feeling for their spouse as they once had, they have fallen hopelessly out of love and nothing can be done to save the relationship. Nothing could be farther from the truth. As a Christian, do not spend time worrying or wondering if you really love your wife—or your husband or your parent or your neighbor. Will to love. Then act. Act as if you did. And God will give you a new power to love. This is how to make love happen. Your feelings will eventually follow your actions. *Your feelings will always follow the set of your will*.

Often people say, "Oh, I just don't feel very spiritual anymore," or "Religious things just don't appeal to me like they used to." So what? So you are aware of a decrease in your feeling level. This is information. It is data you can use to help you realize that you need to set your will again toward a spiritual relationship with God. It tells you that it is time to start acting spiritually, to start doing spiritual things, to make spiritual things happen. Then in their own time the spiritual feelings too will return.

God does not ask us how we feel. He only seeks the daily set of our will toward His. He knows that feelings will then take care of themselves. It is not our responsibility to concentrate on creating good religious feelings in ourselves. It is our responsibility to continue actively to place ourselves in the will of God. *It is the joining of two wills that forms the only true and lasting union*—not just the joining of two sets of emotions or two intellects. Jesus chose to allow His will to be swallowed up in the will of the Father. Perfect though He was, His own emotions at times ran contrary to the will of God. Christ did not *feel* like dying on the cross. His natural and personal wish was to avoid such pain and embarrassment.

Thank God, Jesus was not His emotions. Jesus was not what He felt—or we still would all be lost. *Jesus Christ was what He willed and what He did!* "He went a little farther, and fell on his face, and prayed, saying, O my Father, if it be possible, let this cup pass from me ["God," He was screaming in intense emotional pain, "I do not *feel* like dying for these people, every one of whom appears to be betraying me."]: nevertheless not as I will, but as thou wilt."[6]

Jesus is our ultimate example of how to make spiritual things happen. He made the most important spiritual event in the history of the universe happen—the redemption of the

YOU CAN MAKE IT HAPPEN! 33

human race—not by His emotions or His thoughts but by the exercise of His will!

The point is, if you want to live the Spirit-filled life, if you want to be baptized with the Spirit and fully indwelt with His miraculous presence—it is up to you to make it happen. You cannot wait for the right emotionally charged climate to be created in the church first. You cannot wait for a complete intellectual comprehension of such a deep and mysterious subject—for your mind is not capable of totally fathoming it anyway. You must appropriate it. You must choose it. *Sadly, many do not ever attain the spiritual life and power that is their heritage, because they insist on waiting for God to do through circumstances that which He has already given them the power to do for themselves through the agency of their own will.*

Too many Christians are like ancient Israel at Kadeshbarnea. Oh, they have come out of Egypt all right. They have been converted. They have come out of the bondage of sin. But now they are sitting, camped on the border of the Promised Land. Waiting.

Occasionally someone comes across the border with some of the marvelous fruit of the Spirit from the land of promise. Those waiting get a taste and exclaim how marvelous it is— how wonderful it would be to dwell in the land flowing with spiritual milk and honey. They sense there must be something more to their Christianity. An exciting life of splendor and promise, power and victory is just over the next mountaintop—just over the river Jordan. But they cannot seem to shake off the lethargy that keeps them encamped in the desert. They wait.

Unquestionably it was God's will for Israel to cross into the Promised Land. He had brought them to its very doorstep. He did His part. They failed to do theirs. The greatest blessing of their lives did not become reality, because they did not make it happen. Feelings pulled them back toward the passions and pleasures of Egypt. Logic told them it was impossible to take the land—were there not giants living there? So they did nothing. An entire generation lost its paradise by default. They drifted back into the emptiness, despair, and frustration of the desert for another forty years.

Too many desert Christians today are waiting for spiritual things to happen when they should be making them happen. Every believer has been invited to step into the promised land of the Spirit-filled life. And what a land it is! A spiritual land of Oz! A land of wonder and deepest fulfillment. To enter it is to enter the very territory of God—to move from the barren desert to the fruited plain, from the courtyard of the temple into the Holy of Holies! It is to partake of the divine nature—the very character and personality of Christ!

This promised land offered to Christians today is nothing less than *Christ in you* by the Spirit and *you in Christ,* by your will. This is the ultimate paradise for the believer in this life—the beginning of heaven on earth. "Whereby are given unto us exceeding great and precious promises: that by these ye might be partakers of the divine nature." "For we are made partakers of Christ."[7]

Imagine a man who falls deeply, madly, passionately in love with a beautiful woman. He wants to be with her constantly. He wants to buy her gifts. In fact, he is willing to share with her the very best of what he has. He wants to hold her and touch her. He wants to marry her and live with her forever. He is a very wealthy man, and he tells her she can move into his mansion. He tells her that she is always on his mind—that he dreams of her and longs for her company day and night. He pleads with her to become his bride—to be intimately his physically, mentally, and spiritually.

But the woman replies, with an air bordering on indifference, "Well, I am sure you are a fine person. But I would only be interested in a platonic relationship with you!"

Many Christians have treated God in exactly the same

way. Since Eden the Father has been making impassioned entreaties, calling His people to a relationship of intimate oneness. "They heard the voice of the Lord God walking in the garden in the cool of the day. . . . And the Lord God called unto Adam and said unto him, Where art thou?"[8]

"Thou hast ravished my heart, my sister, my spouse; thou hast ravished my heart with one of thine eyes, with one chain of thy neck. . . . How much better is thy love than wine! and the smell of thine ointments than all spices. Thy lips, O my spouse drop as the honeycomb."[9]

Through the baptism of the Holy Spirit God calls every believer into the deepest intimacy with Himself. Yet many casually say, "Oh, I believe in You, God. You are a wonderful Being. But I am only interested in a platonic spiritual relationship with You. We can relate intellectually—but no intimacy, please." Such linger in the courtyard at a distance when they have been compellingly called into the holy of holies. They camp in the desert when they have been called into the paradise of the promised land. Francis Schaeffer speaks of "the prison of our platonic spirituality."

One verse in the Bible perhaps captures the essence of true Christianity better than any other single reference. "This is life eternal, that they might know thee the only true God, and Jesus Christ, whom thou hast sent."[10] When the Scriptures use the special word here translated *know*, they refer to a very intimate and special friendship.

After Jesus had told His disciples of the tremendous difference the coming of the Holy Spirit would make in their spiritual lives, He said, "Henceforth I call you not servants; for the servant knoweth not what his lord doeth: but I have called you friends."[11]

Called into the throne room to know the very activity of God! Partners and companions with Divinity! Such is the inestimably high and holy privilege of the post-Pentecost believer. God has faithfully done His part. Now, by consciously choosing the Spirit-filled life, by setting the will to respond to the Father's provision, every Christian may make this great promise a living reality.

It is up to you. You can make it happen.* "Now therefore arise, go over this Jordan . . . unto the land which I do give."[12]

---

*In his book *Living in Our Finest Hour* the author describes clearly and in detail the simple steps each person may take to have the assurance of the baptism of the Holy Spirit.

The Breath of Life

And when he had said this, he breathed on them, and saith unto them, Receive ye the Holy Ghost. John 20:22.

It was a great morning—cold, clear, and frosty. The shingles on the farmhouse roof, the trees back in the orchard, and the hay in the field all glistened with ice-crystal diamonds.

The little boy tugged at his grandfather's hand, pulling him over toward the frozen mud puddles that dotted the path to the barn. The old man smiled as the little fellow stomped through the ice, delightedly splashing into the brown water beneath.

As they neared the entrance to the barn, the grandfather reached down deep into a big rain barrel beneath the eaves. He tapped with his fist and then—much to the wonderment of the small boy—brought forth a gleaming, clean sheet of ice as large as a window pane. He handed it to his grandson and said, "Here you go—this is so clean you can even lick it like a popsicle." Then he disappeared into the barn to begin milking the cows.

The five-year-old was fascinated with the way the ice reflected the sun. He twisted and turned it, then began to run his tongue over its smooth, cool surface. All of a sudden his treasure slipped from his mittened grasp and fell to the hard, frozen ground—shattering into a thousand glistening pieces!

Realizing that his grandfather was busy with the cows, the boy decided he would have to get his own replacement from the big rain barrel. Standing on tiptoes, he could just barely peer over its edge. But that was enough to see that there were several magnificent pieces floating on the water's surface about halfway down. Placing his hands on the rim, he pulled himself up the side of the big container until his waist reached its rim. Then he bent over and reached toward the tempting prize. Alas—his fingers were just inches away from a gigantic piece!

Wiggling and squirming a bit, he stretched just a little further and was starting to grip the ice—when it happened! Before he even had a chance to shout for help, he plunged head-first into the cold, dark barrel of ice water! His hands pinned back against his sides by the barrel, his head resting on the bottom, and in water up past his waist, he was completely helpless. Soon everything went black.

Surrounded by the noise of the milking machines and oblivious to the disaster, his grandfather continued working in the barn.

The milk-truck driver whistled to himself as he pulled into the barnyard. He was happy, for he was off to an early start and several minutes ahead of schedule that morning. He jumped out of his big rig, but instead of connecting the hose to the tank right away, he decided to go into the barn and say hello to the farmer.

Casually strolling in through the barn door, the driver hesitated for a moment. Out of the corner of his eye something caught his attention. Something unusual. A pair of little boy's black rubber boots were sticking out of the top of the old rain barrel!

The man spun around in his tracks, ran to the barrel, grasped the legs that were in the boots, and lifted the still form of the child out of the icy water. Stretching him out on the frozen ground, he shouted at the top of his lungs for the boy's grandfather and immediately began giving artificial respiration. Persistently he forced his own breath into the lungs of the motionless little boy. How long the youngster had been under water, the truck driver did not know, but—joined by the anxious grandfather—he kept at his diligent effort until at last there was a bit of movement in the little form. Soon the boy coughed, his eyelids flickered, and he began to revive.

Well, dear reader, someone else would have to have written these pages for you if it had not been for that milk-truck driver sharing his breath of life with me that day—for I was that little boy. I still remember that crystal clear morning and how everything went dark inside that old barrel!

"The Lord God formed man . . . and breathed into his nostrils the breath of life; and man became a living soul."[1]

In the Bible, the same word is used for both "spirit" and "breath"—or breath of life. God clearly wished it understood that it is the Spirit who gives life. "The spirit of God hath made me, and the breath of the Almighty hath given me life."[2] Here both "Spirit" and "breath" come from the same word. This helps us understand something unusual that Jesus did after His resurrection: "And when he said this, he *breathed* on them, and saith unto them, Receive ye the Holy Ghost."[3]

Just as God the Father brought man to life physically for the first time in the Garden of Eden, so Christ bestows the Holy Spirit to bring the believer into fullness of life. Some think the Holy Spirit's filling affects only the spiritual life. Not so. Such a concept sadly limits what God wants to do for the Christian. Paul wrote, "If the Spirit of him who raised Jesus from the dead dwells in you, he who raised Christ Jesus from the dead will give life to your *mortal* bodies also through his Spirit which dwells in you."[4]

Now, one's mortal body is his *physical* being. The Spirit-filled life does not just benefit the spirit of a person—it is also a tremendous healing, life-giving force for the body and mind. I like the way J. B. Phillips translates the above text:

"Once the Spirit of him who raised Jesus from the dead lives within you he will, by the same Spirit, bring to your whole being new strength and vitality."

The Bible promises that the believer is actually given some of the very strength and power of God! "Hast thou not known? hast thou not heard, that the everlasting God, the Lord, the Creator of the ends of the earth, fainteth not, neither is weary? . . . He giveth power to the faint; and to them that have no might he increaseth strength. . . . They that wait upon the Lord shall renew their strength; they shall mount up with wings as eagles; they shall run, and not be weary; and they shall walk, and not faint."[5]

I have often noticed a great difference between elderly people who are dedicated Christians and those who are not believers at all. When people grow older it becomes clear what the set of their life has been. They either tend to become more generous, loving, and kind-hearted with age—or they move in the opposite direction, into self-centeredness, complaining, grouchiness, and pessimism.

You might be able to fake a forced pleasantness at forty or fifty, but by the time you are seventy or eighty most of the veneer has worn off. Masks can no longer hide who and what you really are! To me one of the great proofs of the validity of Christianity and the reality of the indwelling Holy Spirit is the love, gentleness, peace, strength, and vitality evident in the lives of elderly believers.

As a pastor, as a hospital chaplain, as simply a friend, I have held the hands of such people—and touched the hand of God. The presence of the Father and the blessing of the life-giving Holy Spirit rests on such committed believers even in their hour of death. I remember one dear old fellow who used to pray, "Father, keep me alive until I die." And God did. Ponce de Leon went to search for the fountain of youth halfway around the world. All along, it was as close as his Bible—as close as a God "who satisfieth thy mouth with good things; so that thy youth is renewed like the eagle's."[6]

The Bible promises, "as thy days, so shall thy strength be."[7] This was certainly true for Moses—a man who walked very intimately with his God. Though 120 years old when he died, "his eye was not dim, nor his natural force abated."[8]

Naturally, Spirit-filled Christians are still subject to death. But they need not fear old age. They need not fear death. The same indwelling Spirit that had the power to resurrect Christ from the tomb when every devil in hell was trying to keep Him there will one day call them forth to eternity—should life end for them before Jesus comes again. That same indwelling Spirit will strengthen and sustain them through every moment of life in the meantime.

Remember that Paul did *not* say, "Know ye not that your spirit or your soul is the temple of the Holy Ghost?" He said, "What, know ye not that your *body* is the temple of the Holy Ghost which is in you, which ye have of God, and ye are not your own?"[9]

A Spirit-filled person possesses a strength, an energy, a dynamism *physically and mentally* which he would not otherwise have. How marvelous! We offer our weaknesses to Him, and He gives His strength to us! "Blessed is the man whose strength is in thee." "With long life will I satisfy him, and shew him my salvation."[10]

Watchman Nee has written, "The indwelling of the Holy Spirit strengthens our inner man, enlightens the eyes of our heart and makes our body healthy. The power of His life permeates every cell of our being so that we may experience His power and life in the body. No more need we look upon our outer shell as a miserable prison, for we can see in it the life of God being expressed. We now can experience in a deeper way the word which declares that 'it is no longer I who live but Christ who lives in me.' Christ has presently become the source of life to us. He lives in us today as He once lived in the flesh. We can thus apprehend more fully the implication of His pronouncement: 'I came that they may have life, and have it abundantly.' "[11]

You have heard a person described admiringly as "a breath of fresh air," haven't you? Some people just seem to have a sparkle, a dynamic joy, a vitality about them. They bring a refreshing sense of life and excitement wherever they go. People around them feel more alive, confirmed, reassured, and uplifted.

God's intention is to make every Spirit-filled believer a breath of fresh air in the world—and in the church too. Most churches have some stale and musty corners that could certainly use an exhilarating draft of fresh air or a burst of sunlight! Much of our worship has become a rigid ritual. The fresh air of the Spirit breathing on us is needed to turn it into a celebration! Traditional religious habits need to be transformed into vital spiritual experience. The half-hearted mouthing of hymns—done out of habit—as a way to start or end religious meetings needs to be replaced by the joy of what the Bible calls singing "in the spirit."[12]

Whenever the Spirit has been active in great religious movements or activities, a vibrant song has always been heard. Many think of Martin Luther—used of the Spirit in a mighty way to begin the Reformation—as a staid, studious, rather dull theologian who did nothing but pore over his books. But Luther had a deep personal experience with God. And he often expressed himself to God in music, bursting into spontaneous songs of praise, singing with visitors to his home at mealtime, and writing many religious ballads and hymns. The Jesuits complained that Luther's hymns had "damned more souls than his writing and speeches"![13] A historian has said that his chorales "were the fanfare that opened many a Jericho to the advent of the Reformation."[14] He composed the majestic and enduring hymn "A Mighty

Fortress Is Our God," which captures eloquently his spiritual vision and the intensity of his relationship with his heavenly Father.

When revival came to England, John Wesley did the preaching, but the wonderful hymns his brother Charles wrote—as much as anything—brought the wind of spiritual refreshing which swept across the land.

As revival spread to America, Dwight L. Moody—the great evangelist who had received a special bestowal of the Spirit that had transformed his ministry—relied heavily on Ira Sankey, a gifted composer of hymns, to make his large crusades a success. In the early 1900s the evangelist Billy Sunday inspired America with his fervent preaching, but his song leader, Homer Rodeheaver—who conducted the music in the crusades and wrote some of the first modern gospel songs—is just as well-remembered as Sunday. And of course it is impossible to think of the ministry of Billy Graham without also thinking of the deeply spiritual singing of George Beverly Shea.

David, with a heart specially touched by the Spirit, wrote, "Sing praises to God. . . . For God is King of all the earth: sing ye praises with understanding." "Praise the Lord with harp. . . . Sing unto him a new song."[15]

Great sermons, great books, and great hymns are not produced by committees. The Holy Spirit vitalizes individuals. He becomes a great creative force in their lives. He turns ordinary people into extraordinary personalities. He makes them into sparkplugs—people He can use to make things happen for the kingdom of God in the world. These are the kind of people Jesus said would be the salt of the earth. They give flavor and meaning to their own lives and the lives of others.

Every human being is either a positive force for good or a negative force for evil. One thing is certain. You cannot *not* influence! Others are either uplifted or pulled down by every contact they have with you—by the words you speak, the tone of your voice, the very expression on your face. You and I are either becoming a little more like angels or a little more like devils every day, and we are encouraging others by our influence to do the same.

Christ promised a way for every believer to be certain of always having something good and positive to contribute to someone else—of always being a dynamic, creative force for good. To me it is one of the most exciting texts in the Bible: "He that believeth on me, as the scripture hath said, out of his belly shall flow rivers of living water. (But this spake he of the Spirit, which they that believe on him should receive: for the Holy Ghost was not yet given; because that Jesus was not yet glorified."[16]

The best songs are yet to be composed—and Spirit-filled Christians will compose them! The best books are yet to come from the pens of Spirit-filled Christians! The greatest advances in psychology and the science of human relationships are yet to be made—and Spirit-filled Christians will make them! New dimensions of love, joy, and creativity will come from believers filled with the Spirit—for they are to be God's breath of fresh air, His river of living water, in this desolate, dry world.

The Spirit-filled believer always has something good to give. And that is very exciting. That is what living is all about. Too often Christians are known for what they have and what they get rather than what they give. Somehow Christianity has become associated with affluence, in the minds of some people. While the two certainly are not mutually exclusive, and while God puts no halo around poverty, nonetheless things have gone a little too far when some today consider your Christianity deficient unless you are driving a new Lincoln or a Cadillac!

Knowing that I have a background in sales and marketing, a fellow called me the other day, all excited, and said, "I have a new product that is going to be a very good seller, and I want you to handle it for me, because I know you are a go-getter!" I think he thought he was giving me a compliment. But the trouble is that he really wasn't. I want to be known as a great go-giver—not a great go-getter!

The Holy Spirit alone will make you great. Not great in the worldly sense of power or politics or popularity or money or sex-appeal, but great in giving, great in service, great in love. The Holy Spirit alone can make us all we were meant to be. Your own life is, after all, your most creative act. A life lived in love is the perfect work of art! The Spirit-filled Christian may sing the song of life in the key of love!

The Spirit of God is the great regenerative agency in the world today. He is here to breathe life, power, vitality, and creativity into every believer who invites Him into their lives. He is here to dwell in us, to make of our poor, yielded lives a life something like the life of Christ. And this is the ultimate privilege, the ultimate miracle, of our age.

Welcome to the Ministry

Take heed to the ministry which thou hast received in the Lord, that thou fulfil it. Colossians 4:17.

Upon graduating from seminary, I was employed as a church pastor. I was quite pleased at being able to move from the status of a humble seminarian to that of a minister. My position was verified by a very dignified-looking identification card my employer issued to me. This, I was told, was my "ministerial credentials."

I was cautioned to guard this card carefully, for it bestowed certain privileges, responsibilities, and benefits on me. Among the benefits, I was informed, was something called a "clergy discount." Some business organizations and merchants, I learned, offered special reduced prices on their goods and services to preachers.

Delighted to discover this hitherto unexpected blessing, I became intent on taking advantage of it at the first opportunity. Some weeks later I had an afternoon off. I decided to take in a large museum, featuring aircraft exhibits, that I had been wanting to explore for a long time.

Arriving at the entrance, I read the admission prices, which were posted on a large sign. The price of the ticket made me wince. Suddenly it dawned on me—"Why not ask for my clergy discount?" After all, I was in a privileged category now! This seemed like the perfect opportunity to try out the new credentials card I was so proud of and to save some money at the same time.

Turning toward the gate, I became aware that the ticket seller had been watching my hesitation by the sign. He was a burly fellow, about six and a half feet tall. Wearing a striped T-shirt that did not quite succeed in covering all of his big stomach, he reminded me of a professional wrestler. He stood behind the counter with his hands in his pockets, chomping on a cigar as he watched my hesitant approach.

Meanwhile I was busily trying to summon my inner reserves of courage. Straightening my tie, I assumed my most clergylike tone of voice, stepped in front of the counter, and asked as boldly as I could, "Sir, would you please tell me what the price is for a clergy discount ticket?"

The big fellow glowered down at me in silence for a moment. Then, snorting, he bit down on his cigar and said emphatically, "Listen, buddy, we are all Buddhists around here. You ain't no different than anybody else. You pay the same as all the others!"

So came, painfully, my first lesson in spiritual equality!

One of the church fathers, Gratian, once wrote, "There are two sorts of Christians. One clearly of a lower order and weak; the other of a higher order and strong. The first are called laymen; the latter are the clergy." One of Gratian's contemporaries pushed the point a little further. "These two classes are of a totally different order: the one holy and divine, the other human and weak; the clergy are endowed with special gifts and authority; the lower people to do the ordinary work in the world." Naturally, both of these gentlemen were clergymen!

That Christians should be grouped into two categories is not a biblical idea at all. The word *layman* is not even found in the Bible. The word came into religious usage in medieval times. And the concept fit perfectly into the theology of the day, which viewed the priesthood as a highly exalted office.

Pope Boniface VIII, in the year 1302, said in a papal bull,

"The religious sphere is always superior, and the secular, that is the realm of government, of the professions, and of the arts and sciences, is always inferior. For that reason, laymen ought to obey the clergy."

Out of such egomania—out of the darkness and distortion of medieval religion—arose a false distinction between believers. Were it not for the Reformation, there might well be no church, no Christianity at all today. One of the fundamental concepts of Martin Luther's theology was the priesthood of all believers. He wrote, "Christ does not have two bodies or two different kinds of bodies, one secular and one spiritual. Whoever has undergone baptism may boast that he thereby has been consecrated priest, bishop or pope."[1]

To Luther, the Christian alone with his Bible was his own priest. One of his favorite texts began, "Ye are a chosen generation, a royal priesthood."[2] Some accused him of downplaying the importance of the church. Why, after all, was the church important, if believers could approach God on their own? His reply was that the church is important *because* it is made up exclusively of priests! He helped us understand that a priest is also someone who performs religious duties *for other people*. The church is the place God has provided for his priests to be active in personal service to one another and to the world.

Tragically, some of the same old spiritual categorizing and splitting of believers into two classes still occurs today, even as we approach the twenty-first century.

The very forms of worship customary today often facilitate this ecclesiastical elitism. The practice of building a magnificent edifice, lining people up in rows of pews, and keeping them absolutely still while an official clergyman conducts religious ceremonies on a raised platform, came straight out of paganism. Slightly altered by medieval Catholicism, it still influences modern Protestantism today! Though Luther proclaimed the priesthood of all believers

500 years ago, we are still denying it by our traditions, our attitudes, our church architecture, and our churchly forms.

Harvey Cox says, "In their organization, their theology and their ways of relating to the world, our churches today are for the most part merely richer and shinier versions of their nineteenth-century parents. Their organization . . . is based on the sociological patterns of about 1885. . . . Their Sunday-at-eleven culture timed to fall between the two milking hours in the agricultural society. Sermons remain one of the last forms of public discourse where it is culturally forbidden to talk back."[3]

Mark Noll wrote in *Christianity Today:* "Churches are evaluated on the basis of what they can offer us by way of inspiration, warm feelings or entertainment. It is our custom to regard the churches not as centers of interpersonal relationships under the Word of God but as sanctified emporiums competing with weekend camper trips, Little League baseball, and television for the straitened free time of the people. They are places of cooperation where we must be quite careful not to step on anyone's toes lest that person flee to the church down the block."[4]

The baptism of the Spirit alone can endow a man with the power of his own priesthood. The Spirit filling the lives of believers transforms a worship service from a traditional ritual into a triumphant celebration.

Spirit-filled New Testament Christians had no difficulty comprehending that all believers were ministers. Their worship was a shared worship, their ministry a shared ministry. They met in upper rooms, in temple courts, in homes, and even on street corners. Their worship was most of all a time of great joy, spontaneity, and gladness. They experienced a depth of fellowship and support for one another scarcely known today.

Their worship often included eating a full-course meal together and sharing their experiences of an ongoing walk

WELCOME TO THE MINISTRY 51

with God. This was no pious pretense. They unhesitatingly confessed their faults one to another and prayed one for another. They bore one another's burdens.[5] They sang, they prayed, and they praised. Their worship changed them—they never left as they had come in. Those early believers would have a hard time recognizing a traditional Christian worship service today. They would be amazed to witness an audience sitting in silence as a clergyman addresses them, only to be ushered out at the exact stroke of twelve by stoic deacons in three-piece suits!

Dr. Rex Edwards writes that "the New Testament churches were ministering fellowships and in the communities ministering agencies. No difference in rank or status divided the people of God. Church leaders were primarily responsible for preparing the congregation for productive service and witness to the people about them. The church was not viewed as a musical society which hired the performers and sat back to enjoy the performance. The church was an orchestra in which each member was assigned his part to play."[6]

The pre-Reformation church, much to the horror of most modern believers, taught that only the clergy could correctly read or interpret the Scriptures. For this reason the laity was not even allowed to own Bibles for some period of time.

Today we are in danger of returning to this same mentality, because we persist, though in a different way, in separating ourselves—in ranking ourselves spiritually. Today we are more subtle, more sophisticated. We seem to suggest that intellectual training and higher education are the most important requirements for studying God's Word and proclaiming its truth. *When the emphasis on interpreting the Bible is placed on intellectual skills rather than on the indwelling Holy Spirit as the primary guide to truth, then we modern Christians move right back into the old medieval trap!*

A dangerous and divisive tendency today is to select only a few Bible scholars or theologians as being capable and qualified to understand, interpret, and expound the deeper issues of Scripture.

This trend has not only further divided the "laity" from the "clergy" in the church, it has even divided the "clergy" itself into three groups: administrators, theologians, and pastors.

Those without a degree in theology are often left feeling totally inadequate to seek out and understand spiritual truth for themselves. Especially is this the case when they see disagreement among the three above-mentioned groups. They may even notice pastors and administrators beginning to rely heavily on the theologians for biblical interpretation. It is easy, then, for the people in the pews to shrug their shoulders and say, "Well, if those trained in theology cannot seem to find common understanding, how can I ever hope to be able to grasp the meaning of the Bible for myself?"

The whole premise is wrong here. A great difference exists between knowing about God and knowing God. The best-informed theologian on this planet may be the devil himself. He knows more about God than the most brilliant human Bible scholar. But facts and intellectual knowledge are not enough.

Christianity is an affair of the heart, not just the mind. Its reality is not dependent on how well we can systematize or explain it. Though Christianity is comprehended by the mind, its flesh and blood—its beating heart—is a relationship with a real, living Person. No more can it be understood solely by reason or logic than can the love one has for husband or wife, son or daughter. *Spiritual life must never be limited to the intellectually comprehensible!*

The church needs to cease turning to formal religious scholarship as the ultimate interpreter of spiritual truth. Let scholarship make its important, supplementing contribution. But let the believer-priest, alone with his Bible and the guidance of the indwelling Holy Spirit, arrive at his own understanding of truth.

Why are we afraid to trust God? Intellectual agreement and doctrinal harmony do not bring unity among believers, anyway. True unity lies in the fellowship of the Holy Spirit—the only source of true oneness and love among believers.

Jesus Himself promised that after the day of Pentecost, Christians would enjoy a new ability to understand Bible truth. "But the Comforter, which is the Holy Ghost, whom the Father will send in my name, he shall teach you all things." "Howbeit when he, the Spirit of truth, is come, he will guide you into all truth."[7]

F. B. Meyer once wrote that before a person is filled with the Holy Spirit, he will try to understand many religious things with his intellect alone. "But," he wrote, "when the Holy Ghost shall come you shall know all things clearly with the heart. . . . A man is said to reason his way, a woman by the quick glance of her intuition sees what she cannot reason, and she jumps to a conclusion to which her husband reasons his way ten minutes later. So is it with the heart when it is illumined by the Holy Spirit. The pure heart of the believer leaps to conclusions which eye hath not seen, nor ear heard, nor the reason of man conceived. The faculty of knowledge is altered: we no longer seek it by the intellect, but by the heart. *The busy intellectual disputant becomes the deep intuitioner.*"[8]

In the old West a popular saying among those who valued their guns had it that "the good Lord made some men big and some men small, but Mr. Colt made all men equal!" The Holy Spirit is the great spiritual equalizer. He is an equal-opportunity empowering agency! To the minister in the pulpit or the minister in the pew, the pastor or the plumber, the preacher or the painter, He freely offers the same ability to draw truth, insight, and power from the Word of God and to share that Word with others.

The Spirit, living in the heart, breaks down all barriers dividing believers. He offers to each one the gifts necessary to carry on a personal ministry for God.

Many are so conditioned by a false idea of what constitutes a ministry for God that they cannot conceive of it apart from the "clergy."

I once left a position as a paid church pastor in order to move to a growing town where there was no church. I had read Paul's remarks about not building on another man's foundation. I wanted to start a new congregation while I supported myself. Immediately I found myself involved in more different ministries than ever before. I sold Christian books in homes in order to meet people who might be interested in studying the Bible. I gave Bible studies in the evenings. I preached at a service in my home every weekend. And I was also busy writing a Christian book (*Living God's Love*).

While traveling away from home for a few days, I visited a church where I had been a pastor some years before. After preaching at the service, I was accosted in the foyer by a little elderly lady. Grabbing me by the elbow so that it almost hurt, she got right to the point. In a tone that evidenced pity and curiosity, she asked loudly, "Well now, don't you feel terrible about not being in the ministry any more?"

How tragic when believers miss one of the most basic concepts of Christianity—*every Christian is a minister.*

Elton Trueblood once said, "The Reformation under Martin Luther came when the Bible was opened to the common man. A modern reformation will come when the ministry is opened to the layman."

Paul challenged the early Christians to "take heed to the ministry which thou hast received in the Lord, that thou fulfill it."[9]

The Christian life involves us in a profound struggle between the forces of good and evil. It is nothing short of warfare. Can you imagine how much a modern army could accomplish if in battle only its generals did any fighting? What if the troops did not work at all, but once a week they gathered to listen to their generals tell them about the campaign? And before they went home for another six days, the troops would take up a collection to pay the generals for their good work!

A Spirit-filled friend of mine is determined to be in on the action. He is a carpenter and mechanic, but his greatest joy is to share Christ with other people. He lives in a part of the world where a boat is the most common mode of transportation. Often he uses his forty-foot vessel to visit remote camps and settlements to preach and give Bible studies. He calls his ministry the Salvation Navy!

Christianity is not a spectator sport. Have you ever noticed how easy it is for spectators, sitting on the sidelines, to become critical of the players on the field? Alert pastors today realize the tremendous power in a ministry shared with everyone in a church.

Jerry Cook's church had a membership of fourteen people when the idea of a total church ministry involving every member first began to make sense to him. In his book *Love, Acceptance and Forgiveness* he tells how the idea of learning to share the ministry was a struggle for him to accept.

"Our church was at one time very small. I sat around in my office reading and looking busy and hoping something would happen. Some of the concepts of the church-as-a-force had begun to penetrate my mind. I realized that the New Testament teaches that believers are to carry forth the ministry, but I didn't understand how I could get from where I was to where I should be in that regard.

"A phone call came one day from a woman who had been a Christian for only two or three weeks. She said, 'I've been talking to my neighbor and she wants to receive Christ. Could you come and talk to her?' "[10]

Like most pastors, Jerry Cook was eager to respond to such an invitation. After all, wasn't that his job? he reasoned. He was supposed to be the expert at witnessing and evangelizing. He was the one in the church with the degrees in religion. In response to that call he hurried out, jumped in his car, and started for the woman's house. He had not gone very far before he felt God was trying to give him a message. "If you go there, I will honor My word, and on the basis of her trust in Me that woman will be saved— but I will hold you responsible for stealing the reward of one of My sheep," a voice seemed to whisper to him.

Without driving another mile, he turned around and went back to his office. He says, "On the way back I got a short but intensive course in pastor-people relations. I remembered a deep-sea fishing trip my wife Barbara and I had taken recently. She had tied into a shark out there—a big dude about eight feet long. She was having a ball trying to play out that shark. About that time one of the crew members came, took her pole from her and landed the shark for her. What a letdown. He had taken away her victory, and she resented it.

"The Lord said, 'Jerry, that's exactly what you've been doing as a pastor. You have been running in, taking away the ministry of the people, thinking you're doing them a favor. But I am going to judge you for stealing their rewards.' "

Pastor Cook called the woman on the phone. He told her it was not right for him to go and witness to her friend, and he told her why. At first the lady was frightened by the idea of talking to her friend about spiritual things by herself. She argued with the pastor. But eventually she agreed reluctantly to try it herself. The pastor had prayer with her on the phone, and the woman gathered her courage and set off.

WELCOME TO THE MINISTRY 57

Pastor Cook reports the results: "Less than an hour later, there came a knock on my study door. Here stood this woman and her neighbor, both glowing as if they had strobe light on their faces. Not only had the neighbor been gloriously saved, but both women had begun to understand that leading people to Christ is not the exclusive work of a few well-trained professionals."

Using the concept that every Christian is a minister, Jerry Cook has seen his church near Portland, Oregon, grow from fourteen members to over 4500 in a few year's time.

Sadly, many go to church once a week to hear one man exercise his gifts. But the focus of the New Testament church after the Day of Pentecost was to prepare *all* believers to develop their gifts for ministry in the church and in the world.

Paul says that Christ "gave some, apostles; and some, prophets; and some, evangelists; and some, pastors and teachers; for the perfecting of the saints, for the work of the ministry, for the edifying of the body of Christ."[11]

The punctuation of the Bible is not inspired. By removing one comma (which translators of the New English Bible did), it becomes clear that God has given different roles and gifts *for the perfecting of the saints for the work of the ministry!*

Collectively, the sincere believers in the pews are like a great, sleeping giant. They must be awakened to fulfill their ministry and calling as priests of God in their families, their churches, and in the world where they live and work. The "clergy" must not only permit them to do this, it must aggressively lead and encourage them to do it. This should be, in fact, the chief task of pastors and church administrators. The "clergy" must be like John the Baptist—their role must decrease in visibility while that of the "laity" increases. The "clergy" is too often guilty—out of sheer egotism—of jealously guarding the ministry and holding it in reserve for itself. The "laity" has bought into this system; as it has come down from paganism and out of lethargy and indifference it fails to claim its rightful place in the church.

When the ministry is not shared between the pastors and the people, the church suffers. When the ministry is left with pastors and administrators, the church is distorted. It becomes top-heavy. An atmosphere is created in which pastors and church administrators move away from the biblical role of serving the people and become instead a vast spiritual and political hierarchy—a hierarchy that soon comes to exist to support itself. Eventually such a hierarchy can take the form of a sort of spiritual dictatorship, which heavy-handedly begins to exert control over the people in the pew, depriving them of their spiritual freedom, creativity, and spontaneity.

Increasingly this leads the church to focus on its own concerns, needs, and theology and to focus less and less on the needs of the world it was called to serve. This spiritual introversion is often accompanied by a growing intolerance for any deviation from the ecclesiastical or theological norm.

The true character of a church can best be seen in its attitude toward its detractors. Churches which have left the ministry primarily in the hands of the "clergy" often react quite violently and vehemently toward those who dare to challenge it in any way. And this fosters a leadership which tends to be uncaring about individuals and a church government that is self-perpetuating. The ultimate earthly authority of the church must always remain with the whole body of members. The variety of gifts the Spirit-filled life produces in individual believers is vital to the health of the corporate body.

Historically, it has been difficult for a "clergy" directed church to keep before it the sacred vision that it is called to serve, not to rule.

Jesus said to all believers, "Ye have not chosen me, but I have chosen you, and ordained you, that ye should go and bring forth fruit."[12]

WELCOME TO THE MINISTRY 59

Every Christian is ordained—not for rank or position or ecclesiastical power-wielding, but for service. The only authority any minister has—and that includes the minister in the pulpit as well as the minister in the pew—is the authority to serve.

Gottfried Oosterwal writes that "baptism [by water] signifies our ordination to the ministry of Christ. If you are baptized you are made a minister."[13] While water baptism initiates believers into the true ministry, it is the baptism of the Holy Spirit which *empowers and equips* them to carry out that ministry—that special assignment from God.

Christ never intended the gift of the Spirit to be primarily for the purpose of helping to attain perfection, correct a bad temper, or save a floundering marriage. The Spirit certainly works to assist believers with character growth, but this is a quite different work of the Spirit than His work of baptizing them with fire so they can begin a ministry of power and service to the world. "Ye shall receive power, after that the Holy Ghost is come upon you: and ye shall be witnesses unto me . . . unto the uttermost part of the earth."[14]

When I looked for employment as a pastor, the job qualifications seemed to be primarily intellectual. I needed an advanced degree from an approved theological seminary. And as long as I had this, was the husband of only one wife, and was inclined not to teach any heresy, it was assumed that I was qualified for the ministry. Alas, not once was the one, great biblical qualification for the ministry ever mentioned to me as a young pastor. No one bothered to inquire if I had ever experienced a personal encounter with the Holy Spirit. No one ever asked for or invited me to receive the filling of the Holy Spirit by faith.

In college and seminary I learned everything from how to balance the church books to keeping a Volkswagon running so I could make pastoral visits. I learned about the beasts of Daniel 7, the great theologians of the twentieth century, and how to parse Greek verbs. Sadly, the Holy Spirit was never the focus of any course of study. No wonder someone has said that the doctrine of the Holy Spirit is at once the most central and the most neglected doctrine of the Christian faith!

In the New Testament church, the chief criteria for selecting even the deacons was the filling of the Holy Spirit. And their responsibility was only to care for the more practical, physical tasks in the church. Yet the apostles advised, "Brethren, look [pick] ye out among you seven men of honest report, full of the Holy Ghost and wisdom, whom we may appoint over this business. . . . And the saying pleased the whole multitude: and they chose Stephen, *a man full of faith and of the Holy Ghost,* and Philip."[15]

If the apostles assumed that the deacons' ministry would be limited to "waiting on tables," how wrong they were! It is impossible to predict or limit the ministry of a Spirit-filled person. Stephen went on to become one of the greatest witnesses for the Christian faith the world has ever known. Almost immediately, "Stephen, full of faith and power, did great wonders and miracles among the people."[16]

And Philip was not to be left out either! "Then Philip went down to the city of Samaria, and preached Christ unto them. And the people with one accord gave heed unto those things which Philip spake, hearing and seeing the miracles which he did. For unclean spirits, crying with loud voice, came out of many that were possessed with them: and many taken with palsies, and that were lame, were healed. And there was great joy in that city."[17]

The claiming of the baptism of the Holy Spirit by faith simply must be the prime qualification for any person today who desires to have any kind of ministry for God. This qualification has absolutely nothing to do with traditional "clergy-laity" roles. Church officers should be selected not because of incumbency, professional prestige, advanced education, or financial or political leverage—but because they are obviously Spirit-filled and Spirit-gifted.

The baptism of the Holy Spirit can transform one's entire life into a great, sacred adventure. The believer's every word and act can bring glory to God! Such a Christian can be gifted, inspired, transformed! He can catch a vision that allows him to see a ministry for God in even the simplest deed.

Let the good news go out. The priesthood really is for all the people. The veil has been torn down! Every believer may enter into the holy of holies—into the very presence of Almighty God—through the Spirit dwelling within. The one entering this kind of splendid intimacy with God can thereafter do no common act. To the believer who encounters the Spirit, every word and act can become as sacred as a prayer or a communion service. In fact, it is God's intent that being filled with the Spirit should make every Christian's life a living sacrament!

Without this special vision, without the Spirit-given gifts, neither the minister in the pulpit nor the minister in the pew is equipped to serve efficiently. Clearly then, with this essential common source of inspiration and empowerment for all believers, there should be no such categories as "clergy" and "laity" in the church today.

In terms of genuine Christian service there are only disciples. Let us have the courage to be done with this harmful distinction that has only served to shamefully divide the body of Christ and to grieve the Holy Spirit.

Arnold Come has written: "If the mere word laity is preserved at all in our ecclesiastical terminology, all the traditional distinctions between clergy and laity will re-assert themselves. . . .The church is now ready for, and its God-given mission now demands, the complete abandonment of the clergy-laity distinction."[18]

Jesus did not want any discriminatory terms used among

His disciples. Referring to the inauspicious term *rabbi*, which simply means "teacher," He said, "Be not ye called Rabbi: for one is your Master, even Christ; *and all ye are brethren.*"[19]

Nothing written here should be taken to mean that it is inappropriate for an individual Christian to find his place in ministering in the church in the role of a pastor or administrator. However, when he speaks to others in his congregation, let him not stand up and address them as "My dear laymen." Let him address them as *"My fellow ministers."*

The Crucible of Love

And the Lord God said, It is not good that man should be alone; I will make him an help meet for him. . . . Therefore shall a man leave his father and his mother, and shall cleave unto his wife: and they shall be one flesh." Genesis 2:18-24.

Two young Christians, recently married. Both are physicians. She is talented, attractive, athletic. They have laid plans for an exciting future together. Then—a tragic car wreck. The young woman loses both her legs—and an arm.

She calls her husband to her hospital bed. She pleads with him to leave her and never come back. Things can never be the same between them again, she says. He has a whole life of his own to live, and she tells him she does not want to hold him back.

With tears flowing freely her husband begs her not to talk that way. As the long, difficult months go by, he stays near her; daily helping to restore her and give her confidence and courage.

Years pass. Both succeed in their specialty in medicine— the woman practicing from a wheelchair. The husband tells his close friends that he loves his wife now a thousand times more than before the accident.

Love without an if. Love with total commitment. Love that lasts "until death do us part." Love—a special miracle love that exists most deeply between Christian mates. This kind of Holy Spirit inspired love leads a husband to say, "Wife, there is absolutely nothing that can happen to you, nothing you can do or say to me, that could ever possibly make me stop loving you."

This sort of supernatural love is the foundation upon which God chose to create the world and the human race in the world. In His divine wisdom God made the marriage relationship—the family—to be the great crucible of love. When the Father created people, He designed them to be members of families. Thus would their greatest needs be met—their highest purposes fulfilled. The Creator even described Himself once as "the God of all the families of Israel."[1]

Unquestionably the very future of the human race, the well-being of society, and the success of the church all depend on marriage and the family being maintained as the center of love in this world.

Not everyone shares the Christian perspective on the family. Some feel that the family is a relic from the past—that it is even counterproductive. Dr. Ashley Montague once described the family as "an institution for the systematic production of physical and mental illness among its members." Psychiatrist R. D. Laing, who relentlessly carried on a crusade against the family, wrote, "The initial act of brutality against the average child is mother's first kiss."

Philip Larkin penned this ode about the family:

They mess you up, your mum and dad.
They may not mean to, but they do.
They fill you with the faults they had
And add some extra, just for you.
But they were messed up in their turn
By fools in old-style hats and coats.
Who half the time were soppy stern
And half at one another's throats.
Man hands on misery to man.
It deepens like a coastal shelf.
Get out as quickly as you can—
And don't have any kids yourself![2]

THE CRUCIBLE OF LOVE 65

Sadly, some of these observations about the family are at times all too true. Some families feed on their own sicknesses unto the third and fourth generation. Some families turn on and destroy their own members. The family has not escaped sinful man's knack for taking something God-given, sacred, and holy and turning it into a destructive nightmare.

Rather than causing us to give up on the family, this should challenge us to uphold the value, meaning, and dignity of the family all the more. *The fire of God's love must be kept brightly burning in the crucible of the family, or it will go out in all the world.*

The Christian's highest and holiest mission is to make his or her family a bit of heaven on earth, a place of refuge, a radiant center of joy and love. We are the ones most of all called to love—to be experts at loving. This is our mission. And this ministry of love must start with our own families.

When I talk or write about the tremendous power of the baptism of the Holy Spirit to equip believers for an extraordinary ministry of their own, some people think they will be called to take on the city of New York or the continent of Africa. Very unlikely. *A ministry from the Spirit starts with your own husband or wife.*

If you cannot minister Christian love to your spouse, you can have no effective ministry to your children, your church, your neighbor, or the world!

In marriage counseling it is always so sad to hear a person say things like, "Well, my marriage is just not giving me what I need anymore," or, "I am just not getting anything out of our relationship."

To the Christian, a marriage is not primarily a place where you go to get *your* needs met. *A marriage is a place you go—a relationship you have—in which to love and serve and minister.*

Everybody today, including Christians, seems to be asking, "What can my marriage do for me?" They need to start asking, "What can I do for my marriage?—What can I do for my husband, my wife?—What can we two do in our united togetherness for someone else that we could not do alone?"

You see, a Christian marriage is an arena for service—service first of all to your mate. Then, joining with your mate, it becomes a crucible of love and service to your children—and then to the world.

Danger exists in viewing marriage primarily as a place to go to get your needs met. With the depersonalization of the individual, with the loss for many of the extended family nearby, with most people experiencing increasing vocational and financial pressures, a marriage often appears to be the last oasis many have left. It seems to be their last and best hope for love and emotional support in an increasingly uncaring and hostile world.

Never before have so many asked so much of marriage. Christians are doing this too. You go into the average religious bookstore today, and you will often find the largest section—sometimes one whole wall—devoted to books on Christian marriage. Christian marriage has become big business. At least for the book publishers.

In the bookstore sections on marriage there are always a whole host of books on sex. It is almost as if Christians have just discovered sex! Apparently every Christian writer now feels he or she must write a book on Christian sex! It's all there—books on sex and the teenage Christian, sex and the geriatric Christian, born-again sex!

God is certainly the one who invented sex, and sex is certainly to be enjoyed and celebrated by the Christian couple. Certainly it is an important and positive thing to learn to relate to one's mate in any way. I just hope that while we are doing this we do not lose our perspective. I wish we Christians could become as interested and excited about intimacy with God as we have about making sure our intimacy with our husbands and wives is finely tuned.

David spoke of panting after God as the hart pants after the waterbrook. We scarcely know today what that kind of passion for closeness with God is all about.

Christians need to avoid looking to marriage as the ultimate panacea. With all of our marriage-enrichment seminars and our how-to-be-happy-though-married lectures, we may be guilty of a sort of marriageolatry. We are prone to make an idol of marriage if we try to make it more than it is—if we demand more of it than God ever intended.

The message we sometimes seem to be hearing is that "If you only have a good marriage, you can be a good Christian." But good marriages do not make our Christianity. Our Christianity makes our marriages good.

Marriage is good; marriage is very important to people, to society, to the church, and to the world. But *marriage is not sufficient*. Only God is. Marriage cannot meet all our social or emotional or spiritual needs. Only God can.

To see marriage in its true perspective—as an opportunity to minister God's love to your mate, to your children, and to the world—is to catch the true vision of this great gift the Creator gave us in the very beginning. This enhances its value and meaning more than anything else.

Most people agree that the best way for a man to be a good father to his children is for him to love their mother well. *However, it is just as true that if a believer is to be a good minister to the world, he must love his family well.* That is where true priesthood, true Christian ministry to the world begins.

That priorities can be so easily reversed is very unfortunate. The misconception that somehow a believer's marriage or his children must take second place in life to his ministry to others is a grievous error. Some feel it somehow noble or heroic to "sacrifice" their time or involvement with their mate or children in order to give first priority to serving others—the "others" not being located under their own roof, of course. Usually the farther away the "others" are located, the more noble the service is deemed to be!

The baptism of the Spirit is needed to help Christians get their priorities in service straight. God indeed does call men to work for Him in the "uttermost parts of the earth." *But those who are effective for Him there will be effective for Him in their own homes first.*

Believers simply must learn to give first priority in their lives to relationships. A relationship with God first—a relationship with husband or wife, second.

Statistics unblinkingly show that of those who nowadays say, "I do," half—within a few years—will say, "I am through." Sadly, according to recent surveys, the divorce rate for Christians approaches that of nonbelievers.

The failure of a marriage—especially a Christian marriage—is a profoundly serious and tragic thing. It is a failure at loving. Since God is love, it is in one sense a denial of God.

Christ chose marriage to symbolize the deep relationship between Himself and His church. When a Christian marriage falters or fails, it cannot help but depreciate what the Saviour did on the cross. The repercussions of a failed marriage echo into eternity.

God wants to use every marriage to show the world His love. When a marriage fails, He cannot. God wants to use every marriage to introduce the children that come from it to Himself. When a marriage fails, He cannot.

Divorce can be considered as nothing less than the suicide of a relationship. Under most circumstances *couples should no more consider divorce as a solution to their marriage problems than they should consider taking their own lives to end their personal problems.*

God's plan has always been to show the world His love—to reveal the Saviour—through the oneness Christians have with each other. Christian marriage brings the most complete oneness it is possible to experience in this life. When such a marriage fails, it can be a reflection on the very mission of Christ to this world. It can create doubt in other minds that Jesus really is the Saviour. "That they all may be one," He said, "*that the world may believe that thou hast sent me.*"³

Because the spiritual meaning of marriage is so poorly grasped, divorce is no longer seen as the tragedy it really is. Even some believers tend to view divorce now only in terms of its psychological and sociological impact. The question is seldom asked, "Will this belittle or offend Jesus Christ?" or "Will this affect the spiritual life of some other person?"

Instead, the issues commonly addressed are, "Will this affect my job?" "How can I handle living alone?" "What will I do when the car breaks down?" "How will this affect my self-image?" "How do I cope with the guilt?" Or "how will the children's emotional stability be affected?"

While the emotional and social implications of divorce are a legitimate focus of compassion and concern, they must never be allowed to eclipse the fact that the real tragedy of divorce is that it virtually blasphemes the Lord God of heaven. It diminishes the Creator, who gave marriage as a sacred gift to mankind. It diminishes the Saviour, who gave marriage the ultimate compliment of choosing it to symbolize His relationship with His church. It diminishes the Lord, who wanted to use the splendid potential for unity in the relationship to reveal His redemptive divinity to the world.

With the elevation of purely humanistic values of marriage, the door has been opened to many perversions. A spiritual concept of marriage does not allow for such a deviation as homosexuality.

Homosexuality is not so terribly wrong simply because of

its physical or psychological implications. It is a sin because of its *spiritual* implications. It is most of all a blasphemy against God. It is man saying, "I'll do it my way." It is a denial of the Creatorship and sovereignty of God. It is a Satanically inspired insult against the Saviour—the divine Bridegroom—who claims that fair woman, His church.

When abortion is considered only in the light of the psychological and sociological effects it may produce, no clear-cut case can effectively be made against it, either. Only when clearly viewed from the perspective of divine love and law can its true heinousness—its departure from God's will—be grasped.

Spirit-filled Christians who cherish the sanctity of the family, the sacredness of sex, and the supremacy of love cannot possibly countenance either homosexuality or abortion when the mother's life is not in danger.

Some say, "Oh, we are not pro-abortion, we are just pro-choice." Ever since Eden, Satan has been whispering that people have the right to be "pro-choice." The Religious Coalition for Abortion Rights has stated, "Abortion is an individual decision, and therefore your God-given right."

I do not know of any Christian church or group which is pro-choice on child abuse or incest. No reputable group of Christians would say to one of its members, "Well, Sister Jones, we don't think you should go to bed with your neighbor's husband, but you are entitled to make up your own mind about it, because we are pro-choice!"

Some groups hold that the church has the right to hold certain enforceable standards as to what a believer should wear, what he should eat, and what forms of entertainment he may enjoy, yet amazingly enough some of these same groups are pro-choice on abortion! They say, "It's up to you whether you abort your baby or not, because in our church we respect an individual's freedom of choice!"

Without the perception given by the indwelling Spirit,

even believers can lose sight of the true meaning of love and marriage and family. "The fruit of the Spirit is love," and unless one has this supernatural love he cannot discern what is right or wrong in relationships. He cannot even love his own wife and children unconditionally.

Unconditional love goes beyond three-tiered wedding cakes and love-boat honeymoons and marriage contracts. Unconditional love is a God-given ministry to another person!

"Alas," some say, "such love is a wonderful ideal, but in this sinful world it is impossible to achieve." The Holy Spirit, however, is in the business of making the impossible dream the possible reality—the ordinary, the extraordinary—through the infusion of the divine nature into the human!

Instead of the church simply growing more alarmed at the increasing number of broken homes—instead of struggling merely to treat the growing number of human emotional and psychological needs, let it do something more. While doing the above is appropriate, Christians must be very careful not to get so caught up in treating the symptoms of the disease called lack of love that they fail to offer the cure!

The church must not forget that its primary mission is to share the miracle—the miracle that "the love of God is shed abroad in our hearts by the Holy Ghost which is given unto us."[4] It can speak authoritatively of a love that knows no limit to its endurance, no end to its patience.

Let the church at the close of the twentieth century not lose sight of its priorities. Let it not get caught up in making excuses for less-than-moral, less-than-loving behavior. Let it not get caught up in band-aiding the world's hurts when it could be offering the rich healing of the love of God through the Holy Spirit.

When the Spirit-filled disciples were asked by the lame man at the temple gate for some money, they could have probably produced a coin or two from the deeper recesses of their robes. They could have tossed these in the man's lap so he could have bought a crust of bread. Better yet, they could have sat down and practiced their best psychological technique on him. They could have said, "Well now, tell us, Brother, just what does it feel like to be lame? You must feel very frustrated at times, very alone, very left out."

Nothing is wrong with giving a beggar a coin or a piece of bread. Nothing is wrong with listening and being sympathetic to the problems of a cripple. Sometimes this is all that can be done. But if—if you can do *something more*—?

"A certain man lame from his mother's womb, seeing Peter and John about to go into the temple asked an alms. And Peter, fastening his eyes upon him with John, said, Look on us. And he gave heed unto them, expecting to receive something of them. Then Peter said, Silver and gold have I none; but such as I have give I thee: In the name of Jesus Christ of Nazareth rise up and walk."[5]

God gave the Holy Spirit to the church so that it could do "something more." So that it could be "something more." Something more in men's hearts, in their marriages, in their families, and their workplaces.

Believers today are living 2000 years on the down-love side of the cross. This *is* Christianity's finest hour. We have had the benefit of centuries of study and exploration of the Scriptures. We have had the Spirit's leading into new truth, new life, new power. We should be the finest, lovingest, highest-idealed, most problem-solving, healing group of people this planet has ever seen!

For example, when it comes to marriage, instead of believers getting caught up in so much prurient worrying about who the "innocent" and "guilty" parties are in a divorce, let them be concerned with setting the standards of Christian behavior and marriage higher than they were in Jesus' time.

After all, those who lived before the cross—before the

day of Pentecost—did not have as much Spirit-revealed knowledge on many questions as we do today.

When Christ said that a person could divorce his mate on grounds of adultery, He was not necessarily approving an ideal and permanent norm for believers for the next 2000 years. He was speaking to a given problem at a given point in time. He was improving radically on the standard of the day. Then, a man could divorce his wife for no reason at all, simply by writing her a note!

Christ never openly opposed slavery in His time. Yet today it would be a sin for Christians not to have a higher standard—not to condemn it.

The unfortunate tendency of late has been for believers to set standards as low as they can be and still be biblical. Why not set standards as high as they can be? In this, love's power will be given a chance to show that it is sufficient for all things.

When the Bible says that love can "endure all things," it does not exempt caring for an "unexpected" child. It does not say love is powerless to compensate for a pull toward a homosexual or inappropriate heterosexual relationship. It does not say love can handle everything thrown at it except "incompatability" or "mental cruelty"—or even adultery— in marriage.

Instead of believers seizing upon adultery as an excuse to end a marriage, let it more often be regarded as one more opportunity for love to show its supremacy over absolutely everything.

The Spirit-filled life also gives a whole new dimension to the ministry of parents to their children. Implicit in the concept of every Christian as a minister is the priesthood of the father in the home. The average male parent does not realize that his first responsibility to his family is spiritual, not financial. "Fathers, provoke not your children to wrath: but bring them up in the nurture and admonition of the Lord."[6]

Outside the church the concept of true fatherhood has been mostly abandoned. Many parents devote the best years of their lives and their children's lives to "getting ahead." Often they claim to be "doing it for the family."

A Christian priest-father must be certain his priorities are right. He must have the Spirit living in him, so that he abandons the natural order of human motives and goals. Dr. Ross Campbell, in his excellent book *How to Really Love your Child,* says, "Real happiness is found in family orientation—spiritual family, then physical family. God, spouse, children, these are essential. The remaining priorities are important, but these must come first."[7]

Frequently I have heard many parents over the age of forty express the regret that they did not spend enough time with their children when they were young. They sense that they missed out on something beautiful—something special and sacred. The "what might have beens" still haunt them.

Determined that this would not happen in our family, my wife and I sold a business we had in a large city just when it was beginning to prosper. We moved to a wilderness lake, built a home, and spent several years devoting our lives almost exclusively to our two children. We worked together to earn a living, we hiked, we worshiped, we traveled, we played, and we taught them their school work by correspondence courses. It was a most wonderful time. We could sense God's blessing over our family. Even today, with the children almost ready for college, we all look back on those years with great joy. Something good happened that will always be a part of all our lives.

Today, with the father's role commonly recognized as mainly a provider, with more and more mothers seeking "personal fulfillment" and "self-expression" in careers outside the home, the challenge lies before every Christian parent not to abandon sacred priorities. Fathers may need to change their life-style so they can have more quality time with their children. Mothers may need to postpone for a few years the development of their own careers.

A lot is said about equal rights today. But the equal rights believers should be most concerned about are the equal rights of every Christian to minister, to serve, and to love. The demonstration the world most needs to see is not composed of signs and placards, but a convincing demonstration that Christianity really produces better people, better husbands and wives, better fathers and mothers.

Earlier, Peter was quoted as saying, "Silver and gold have I none, but such as I have give I thee." Your child does not need your money or all the fancy trappings of twentieth-century merchandise nearly so much as he needs you. You may not have much wealth to give him, but you can share with him the most valuable thing you possess—your time.

In this way you minister to him in the most important manner possible. When you give your child your time, you are literally giving him your life. By this you show your child the measure of his worth to you. What you do with your time sends a very clear message to your child, whether you realize it or not.

You also minister to your child by giving unconditional love. To show a youngster what God is like, you must love him or her without an "if." This means accepting the little one warmly, regardless of what he does or who he looks like or what he is. Though there will be times you must discipline, the youngster still needs to know there is absolutely nothing he can do or say that will prevent you from loving him.

Your child needs to sense that he is so important to you that you would not hesitate to give your life for him.

A parent must also minister to a child a sense of the youngster's own worth. Every child deserves his dignity. He needs to be shown again and again that he is special, unique, cherished—the only one of his kind. Dr. Kay

Kuzma, a parenthood specialist, has written, "The most important thing in a child's life is what he thinks about himself. If a child feels good about himself because his parents have loved, encouraged and given him a sense of self-worth, then he has a healthy attitude toward life and is able to cope with various levels of life problems."

For the Christian, the worth of his child is not first established sociologically or biologically or even emotionally—but spiritually. The Bible says plainly, "Lo, children are an heritage of the Lord."[8]

The Spirit-filled parent is given the vision to see that his child is not really his own at all. A child is a sacred trust from God. Christ gave one of His most shocking and severe warnings to those who might not be faithful in their ministry to their children. "As for the man who is a cause of stumbling to one of these little ones who have faith, it would be better for him to be thrown into the sea with a millstone round his neck."[9]

The Holy Spirit enables the Christian to keep on seeing his child as a treasure from the Lord. This special perspective makes it possible for the parent to have the same role Mary did in raising the Son God gave her.

The greatest ministry of parents today is to bring up children to live God's love and truth as Jesus did. While children are not born with a divine nature, under the guidance and loving care of Spirit-filled fathers and mothers, they can have the very nature of God available to work in their lives. It has been said that if there were more mothers like Mary, there would be more children like Jesus!

Christian parents have a wonderful heritage to share with their children: the treasures of the Bible, the ministry of angels, the assurance of salvation—and that heaven might begin here on earth—the filling of the Holy Spirit. "Ye shall receive the gift of the Holy Ghost. For the promise is unto you, *and to your children.*"[10]

Take Your Love to Town

The fruit of the Spirit is love. Galatians 5:22.

I was a typical eight-year-old—a skinny legged little kid with a face only a mother could love. I was about as cute as a can of worms! I had a thick thatch of red hair that seemed determined to hang down in my eyes—and freckles! Enough freckles to make Sunny Jim eat his heart out!

That summer long ago, something special was going on in the little Alaskan village that was our home. A church that operated a mission station there was putting up a new building. Because it was difficult to get help in such a remote location, pastors from other states had been invited to come north and donate their time in erecting the building.

One afternoon in the middle of the project it was decided that the men would take a break and go swimming. I had been hanging around the site watching and undoubtedly making a pest of myself, yet someone was charitable enough to invite me to tag along. I was all excited about being included with the men and could hardly contain myself on the long walk to the pond that served as the local swimming hole.

By the time we arrived, evening was approaching. What warmth the sun had generated was fast disappearing. Though Alaska is far from being a land of perpetual ice and snow, nonetheless its bathing beaches are not exactly tropical!

The temperature of the water did not cool the enthusiasm of the men, however. Soon they were in the water, hollering and splashing and having a great old time. And I was too—for awhile. But then the cold water began to get to me. Of course I wanted to be brave like the big fellows. So I hollered and splashed too. But I was just a skinny little kid, and I kept getting colder and colder.

Finally, I could stand it no longer. I had to get out. My lips were turning blue, and I was shaking so badly I could barely walk. By now the sun had disappeared behind a hill. I had no towel. In my eagerness to get into the water I had left my clothes by the shore. And now they were soaking wet from all the splashing.

I stood there on the bank by myself, not knowing what to do. I did not even really know any of the men with whom I had come, and I was getting increasingly colder. I did not know the way back home. Great shakes and shudders were beginning to pass through my little frame. My knees were knocking, and my teeth were chattering. The only warm thing about me were the great big tears that were starting to trickle down my freckled cheeks.

Then all of a sudden—from somewhere behind me—appeared a gigantic, fluffy towel. A pair of strong arms reached around me and tucked me into it. I was so wrapped up that at first I could not even turn around to see who my benefactor was. The strong arms began to rub the towel briskly over my chilled little body.

When some of the shaking stopped, I could turn and look at my rescuer. He was a man I did not know at all. He had arrived on the crew only the day before.

He did not go back into the water with the others but stayed with me and helped me wring out my clothes. He too became quite cold and was beginning to shake himself, but he let me keep his towel. Then he even added his own coat over the top of it!

When the others were ready to go, he walked beside me down the trail. He stayed right with me until we were at the door of my home—which took him some distance out of his way. Then, with a smile and a wave of his hand, he went back to join the others.

I am not sure, in my childish embarrassment, if I even remembered to thank him. But I have not forgotten that day—or the man who made it stay so vividly in my mind. Later on, when I learned that he was a pastor, I became one little boy who was very high on pastors!

In fact, not many days had gone by before I decided that I wanted to be a pastor someday too. I knew I wanted to grow up to be someone who would spend his life doing loving things for others.

You see, that one act of unconditional love made a lasting impact on my life. Love is like that—warm and simple as the sharing of a big, fluffy towel, yet so splendid, so ongoing in its power for great good.

One act of love can make a great difference. That man did not know me. He did not know my parents. He had nothing to gain by what he did. I had done nothing to deserve his special care. Yet he loved. Simply because a small, sad boy had a need.

The Bible stands in awe of great acts of unconditional love. Its very focus is on such acts. Especially the greatest act of unconditional love of all time—the one best symbolized by a cross.

For the Spirit-filled Christian, one thing is certain—the bottom line is love. Not just love the emotion, or love the word, or even love the principle, but love expressed in action.

All the theology in the world, all the quoting of Bible texts, all the fervent religious meetings, even all the talk about the baptism of the Holy Spirit means absolutely nothing unless the end product is more love in the life. Religion without practicing, practical, unconditional love is a counterfeit.

This is love that you do, not just love that you feel. This is love with skin on it. Love in bib overalls, cutting an old lady's firewood. Love in Nike running shoes. Love in Calvin Klein jeans! Love that is not afraid to get its hands dirty. Love that sets up a shelter for AIDS victims. Love that takes a risk. Love whose best definition is doing or saying what is for the best good of another person—now and eternally—regardless of how you feel toward him or what you think of him.

The apostle John wrote, "My children, love must not be a matter of words or talk; it must be genuine, and show itself *in action*."[1]

The greatest adventure in life is to experience the love of God in Jesus Christ and to share this marvelous gift with others. In fact, this *is* life itself. If you are not loving, you are not whole. If the books you read, the friends with whom you regularly associate, the church you attend do not in some way move you deeper into experiencing and sharing God's love, they are wasting your time.

In performing acts of love, the Spirit-filled life finds its highest and best expression. If you are expecting the outpouring of God's Spirit to be focused on spectacular spiritual and physical phenomena, you will be sadly disappointed. Astounding events certainly do occur when the Spirit is working, *but the greatest miracles will be simple, quiet miracles of unconditional love.*

Big, warm towels wrapped around cold little boys. A quiet word of understanding, spoken at just the right time when someone is hurting. A gentle touch on the arm as you speak to someone. Holding your own feverish, fretting child as he whimpers at 3:00 a.m.—when you have to get up at 6:00 a.m. to go to work. Saying nothing hostile when your mate comes down on you unfairly. Listening—yes, just listening—with ears of love. Listening when you would rather be talking.

One of the sins of which most Christians are guilty is "overtalk." Jesus said something about letting your conversation go with a simple Yes or No. He knew that we are not what we say. *We are what we do!* At the end of each day, ask yourself, "What have I done today to show my love by my actions?"

I have been writing and speaking about the special subject of the Holy Spirit's baptism for ten years now. People often expect me to talk about the gift of tongues. They seem to think that is very important. Well, it is not. Even Baalam's donkey had the gift of tongues! Tongues are not any big thing. The Bible calls them the least of the gifts. What I covet for myself is the gift of ears! Listening to what people are really saying. Listening to their hearts, not just to their words. Listening with the ears of love. I would like to start a revival in my church. I can see the headlines in my church paper now—"Pentecost Returns—Thousands Receive the Gift of Ears!"

The real ministry to which every Spirit-filled Christian is called, gifted, and empowered is the ministry of love. In a Kenny Rogers song, the poor, paralyzed husband begs Ruby not to take her love to town. Well, fellow Christians, God is begging us *to* take our love to town! He wants us to let our love go public! He wants us to take it, in the power of the Spirit, into the mall at Macy's. To the grocery check-out stand—and into McDonald's. Maybe even into the tavern or pawn shop on First Avenue. And to church too! It is surprising how easy it is to forget to take your love to church. Churches seem to be such private places these days. Private people drive in their private cars to their private churches. They sit in their private spaces and think their private thoughts, listening privately to the sermon. They get back in their private cars and drive to their private homes, where they go on with their private lives! That's not Christianity. That is not even good paganism! Even the pagans had sense enough to have a good time when they got together!

Privacy has become one of our modern idols. Many Christians allow it to quench the Spirit. People say, "Oh, I am a very private person," as if that were some great virtue. It is not a virtue. It is a disease—a social disease. Christians are to be the most open, most public people of all with their love.

Some Christians are actually starting to say nowadays, "Oh, I don't talk about my religion. It is a very private area of my life." Can you believe it? We are starting to treat our Christianity as we used to treat our sex life! Believers now are talking about their sex lives in public and keeping their Christianity private!

To have a ministry of love, you must be open. You must be vulnerable in order really to love. That means you may be hurt or rejected or laughed at or ignored. But you must be vulnerable to be a Christian. No vulnerability, no love. It is that simple. Vulnerability is, in fact, the stage that love dances on.

Jesus Christ was a very public person. Even his birth was a public event. Shepherds, wise men, and stable attendants were on hand even before the manger was cleaned up! He gave street urchins free access to His lap—and to His heart. Beggars and lepers and former ladies of the night touched Him. He wept in public. He lived always with his arms wide open to everyone. He even died in public. He hung naked before a curious crowd. He was of all men most vulnerable. He took His love to town. To Jerusalem town. And then to a hill called Calvary.

To say we are shy, to say we are private by nature, is simply another excuse for not loving. *And a failure at loving is the greatest tragedy of all!* Soren Kierkegaard once wrote, "To cheat oneself out of love is the most terrible deception.

It is an eternal loss for which there is no reparation either in time or in eternity."

Another thing we let get in the way of our loving is our theology. A correct theology is not a substitute for a ministry of love. Believers spend a lot of time talking theology. We need to get off the theology boat and get on the love boat! That makes the two sound as if they are mutually exclusive. They are not. Because the best theology—regardless of the doctrine—centers on love.

Once I gave a weekend seminar on "Living God's Love." I was preaching my heart out on love, and after one meeting an older brother came up to me. I could tell by the look in his eyes that I was in trouble. He said, "All this love stuff is OK, I guess, but when are you going to preach us some good, solid doctrine? You haven't said a thing yet about the judgment or the mark of the beast or Armageddon!"

I respectfully submit to you, dear reader, that love *is* our highest and best doctrine, our finest theology. John wrote, "If we love one another, God dwelleth in us, and his love is perfected in us."[2] Now that is real theology.

If love is the center of your life and your religion, it can make up for a great many other things you do not have. If you do not have love at the center of your life, no matter what else you have, you will never have enough. Even the Bible says that love covers a multitude of evils. That does not mean you have a license to sin. What it *does* mean is that you have a license to love!

Pure doctrine does not unite believers nearly so much as does a fellowship of love in the Holy Spirit. In fact, doctrine—emphasized without love—can only lead eventually to alienation. Every church which is going to maintain its existence must decide at some point which of these two will receive the higher priority—which will be the center of its heart and soul and worship. The choice is ever whether to put doctrinal harmony and purity first or to put unity and oneness and accepting love between members first.

To some people, love is something you take time for after everything else is done. Sort of like recreation. They see it as an easy, natural part of living. Christians seems to feel it is something they will do automatically, just because they go to church. Very few people realize the truth about love. *Loving is the hardest work in the world. In fact, the most loving thing you ever do in your life will probably be the hardest*. That is the way it was for Jesus.

People need to start taking their loving seriously. After all, the ultimate success of your life will not be judged by those who admire you for your accomplishments but by those who attribute their wholeness and happiness to your really loving them. Another reason to love seriously is that you cannot possibly love God any more than you love the person you like the least! Your love for God and your relationship with Him is deeply affected by how well you relate to other people. The Bible says, "If a man say, I love God, and hateth his brother, he is a liar: for he that loveth not his brother whom he hath seen, how can he love God whom he hath not seen? And this commandment have we from him, That he who loveth God love his brother also."[3] In deep and wonderful ways, the Father is so close, so much a part of each human being He has created, that the way we treat other people is the way we treat God.

Love must also be taken seriously because *you cannot love the person nearest and dearest to you any more than you love the person you like the least*. The brotherhood of man is not just a theoretical idea. We have such oneness with other human beings that *if you refuse to love your enemy, your neighbor, or your brother, it will eventually set you up to fail at loving someone very near and dear to you*. How well you love your enemies has very much to do with how well you love your own children!

The oneness of all mankind is an exciting frontier that Spirit-filled Christians should be exploring. Edward Carpenter wrote, "If I did not know that the craziest sot in the village is my equal, and were not proud to have him walk with me as my friend, I would not write another word—for this is my strength."

Dr. Leo Buscaglia says that the man who dedicates himself to love as Jesus did "must reject no man, for he realizes that he is a part of every man and to reject even one man, is to reject himself."[4] I would add that for the Christian to reject even one man is to reject God. Love and God are one. To reject one is to reject both. To discover either is to begin experiencing both!

If believers are really going to prove to the world that the last Christian did not die on the cross, they are going to have to prove it by their loving of other people. You see, Jesus Christ did not die on the cross just to restore man's broken relationship with God. He died also to restore the broken chain of love between people. The Saviour came to reconcile us to God *and to each other!*

Salvation is, more than anything else, a restoration of love. Love between people and God—and between people and people. Redemption does redeem us from sin, but in its final definition sin is the absence of love. Redemption, then, is not so much a matter of taking something evil from us as it is restoring back to us something very precious and good that we have been missing.

The love God gives us to share demonstrates that we are Christians—that we are saved. No wonder Jesus said that by this love the world would know we are His disciples. Reconciliation between people is the true sign of Christ's presence—the true evidence of the baptism of the Holy Spirit.

The special, supernatural, unconditional love the Spirit-filled Christian is called to live in this world never loves in order to be loved. It loves simply to love. In the church, too many attempts are made to love with strings attached. To "love" someone simply to make a convert to your church of them is absolutely unethical. That is not love—it is religious manipulation. The Christian is called to love. Period. No strings attached.

We have been so corrupted by Hollywood "love" and Madison Avenue "love" and Jesus-won't-love-you-if-you-hit-the-kitty-cat "love," that we can scarcely comprehend a love that has absolutely no ulterior motive. Such love exists only to minister, to serve, to care. The non-Christian is unable even to conceive of this kind of love. To him it is utter foolishness. But it is where the power in Christianity lies!

This love is a radical and revolutionary force. It is a supernatural gift from the Holy Spirit—God's best gift to humanity. It is so holy and sacred we almost need to take off our shoes before we talk about it. It is so entwined with the character and personality of the heavenly Father that you cannot write or speak of it without talking about God! It is love without an "if." It can outlast absolutely everything. And it can say, "There is *nothing*—absolutely nothing—you can do or say to me that would ever make me stop loving you."

The couple had been married twenty-three years. The husband was sent to the Orient by his employer. He and his wife had always been close. At first he wrote every day. Then once a week. Then the letters came only rarely. Finally they stopped altogether. He did not return home as scheduled at the end of the year.

Then the wife learned the truth—her husband had taken his Oriental housegirl to be his partner, after getting a mail-order divorce. The wife continued to write often, but seldom was there a response. She was informed when a child was born to the couple, and a year or so later another had arrived, she was told.

One day a letter came from across the sea, and she opened

it eagerly. But it bore the sad news that the man she had loved so much was dead of lung cancer. Time passed, but the woman could not get the Oriental girl and those two children out of her mind. Realizing that children of mixed blood could face a very difficult future in their homeland, she wrote the mother, inviting her to send the youngsters to the States. Sensing what an opportunity this could be for her children, the girl agreed. The money for tickets was sent, and the two children came to a new home in America.

The youngsters adjusted quickly. It was a happy time for them and for the woman who had been alone for so many years. But letters from across the sea made it clear how lonely the young mother was. The woman in America made a decision. She must send for the children's mother too. Dipping into her limited savings, she sent another ticket across the sea.

When the plane arrived in New York that day, the last person off was a girl so thin and small that the woman who had come to greet her thought at first she was a child. She quickly took her into her arms. The Oriental girl was welcomed into her heart and into her home.

The years go by. The two children grow up in an atmosphere of acceptance, warmth, and love. They refer to the one woman so important in their lives as mother—the older woman so special to them, they call auntie.[5]

What an example of love without an "if"! Such love is not logical. Most people cannot understand it. They walk away from it shaking their heads. They find it nearly impossible to imagine someone loving like that, when it is not expected of them. But the best kind of love is the love given when it is not expected. Such love is a very radical thing in this unloving world. It is a revolutionary force. This is the love that has spoken worlds into existence and has created a million suns. Love is what makes God all powerful—not force.

The power of God's radical, unconditional love reached down to offer redemption to a lost race on a lost planet. Jesus Christ loved you and me so deeply that He actually risked not being God anymore. That was the ultimate risk of all time. That kind of vulnerability is what bought eternal life for you and me. Love created us. Love has redeemed us. No wonder then that for the Christian, to live is to love and to love is to live. We have been loved so much that we are compelled to love in return. We dare not build our Christianity around anything else.

The church today often finds it easy to concern itself more with issues than with people. This is tragic, for it takes away the emphasis on love. Jesus calmly let the scribes and Pharisees argue over the nuances of their doctrine. He concentrated on expressing love—touching, listening, healing, caring. The time has come for believers to refocus on love. Too long we have talked about love as a philosophy, love as a principle, love as an ideal. We have preached about it and written books about it. The time has now come for us to stop just agreeing with love, believing in love, and discussing love. We must now begin to take a whole new bold initiative in loving. We must become much more aggressive with our love than ever before. Our generation is called *to make love happen* as no other group of people has ever done. Our mission is to love extraordinarily! If we are to succeed at this high calling, our only hope is a new, bold emphasis on the filling of the Holy Spirit—the Source of all such love. "The love of God is shed abroad in our hearts by the Holy Ghost which is given unto us."[6]

When eternity dawns and the struggle is ended—when the last word is spoken of the last generation on earth—may it be said of those of us who lived for God at the end of the twentieth century—"How splendidly did they love!"

References

Games Christians Play

1. Eric Berne, M.D., *Games People Play* (New York: Ballantine Books, 1964), pp. 149, 155.
2. Ellen G. White, *Selected Messages*, bk. 1 (Washington, D.C.: Review and Herald Publishing Association, 1958), pp. 156, 157.
3. See Matthew 3:11.
4. Acts 19:2, RSV.
5. Acts 19:6, RSV.
6. Ted W. Engstrom, *The Pursuit of Excellence* (Grand Rapids, Mich.: Zondervan Publishing House, 1982), pp. 15, 16.
7. Isaiah 40:31.
8. Acts 1:8.
9. John 16:7.
10. Ephesians 2:22, emphasis supplied.
11. 1 Corinthians 6:19, emphasis supplied.
12. Ephesians 1:13, 14.
13. Ellen G. White, *The Acts of the Apostles* (Mountain View, Calif.: Pacific Press Publishing Association, 1911), p. 52.

Poor Man, Rich Man

1. Romans 8:16, 17.
2. Luke 3:23, 22.
3. Acts 10:38.
4. Luke 4:14.

5. Luke 4:18, 19.
6. Luke 4:32.
7. John 14:12.
8. See John 16:7.
9. Romans 8:14-17.
10. John 14:16; 16:7, emphasis supplied.

You Can Make It Happen!

1. Adapted from the book *The Pursuit of Excellence* by Ted Engstrom. (Grand Rapids, Mich.: Zondervan Publishing House, 1982), pp. 23, 24.
2. See John 7:17.
3. Colossians 1:26, 27.
4. Watchman Nee, *The Spiritual Man*, vol. III (New York: Christian Fellowship Publishers, Inc., 1968), p.75.
5. *Ibid.*, p. 84.
6. Matthew 26:39.
7. 2 Peter 1:4; Hebrews 3:14.
8. Genesis 3:8, 9.
9. Song of Solomon 4:9-11.
10. John 17:3.
11. John 15:15.
12. Joshua 1:2.

The Breath of Life

1. Genesis 2:7.
2. Job 33:4.
3. John 20:22, emphasis supplied.
4. Romans 8:11, RSV.
5. Isaiah 40:28-31.
6. Psalm 103:5.
7. Deuteronomy 33:25.
8. Deuteronomy 34:7.
9. 1 Corinthians 6:19.
10. Psalms 84:5; 91:16.
11. Watchman Nee, *The Spiritual Man*, vol. III (New York: Christian Fellowship Publishers, Inc., 1968), pp. 196, 197.
12. 1 Corinthians 14:15.
13. H. G. Koenigsberger, *Luther, A Profile* (New York: Hill and Wang, 1973), p. 226.

REFERENCES 91

14. U. S. Leupold, ed., *Luther's Works, Liturgy and Hymns*, vol. LIII (Philadelphia: Fortress Press, 1965), p. 195.
15. Psalms 47:6, 7; 33:2, 3.
16. John 7:38, 39.

Welcome to the Ministry

1. Martin Luther, *To the Nobility of the German Nation*.
2. 1 Peter 2:9.
3. Harvey Cox, *The Secular City* (New York: Macmillan and Co., 1965).
4. "Believer Priests in the Church: Luther's View," *Christianity Today,* 26 October 1973, p. 4.
5. See James 5:16; Galatians 6:2.
6. Rex Edwards, *Every Believer a Minister* (Nashville: Southern Publishing Association), p. 7.
7. John 14:26; 16:13.
8. F. B. Meyer, *The Christ Life for Your Life* (Chicago: Moody Press), p. 103.
9. Colossians 4:17.
10. Jerry Cook, with Stanley C. Baldwin, *Love, Acceptance and Forgiveness* (Ventura, Calif.: Regal Books, 1979), pp. 67-69.
11. Ephesians 4:11, 12.
12. John 15:16.
13. Gottfried Oosterwal, *Insight,* 6 November 1973, p. 18.
14. Acts 1:8.
15. Acts 6:3, 5, emphasis supplied.
16. Acts 6:8.
17. Acts 8:5-8.
18. Andrew Come, *Agents of Reconciliation* (Philadelphia: Westminster Press, 1966), p. 99.
19. Matthew 23:8, emphasis supplied.

The Crucible of Love

1. Jeremiah 31:1.
2. Salvador Minuchin and H. Charles Fishman, *Family Therapy Techniques* (Cambridge, Mass.: Harvard University Press, 1981), pp. 263, 264.
3. John 17:21.
4. Romans 5:5.
5. Acts 3:2-6.

6. Ephesians 6:4.
7. Ross Campbell, *How to Really Love Your Child* (Wheaton, Ill.: Victor Books, 1977), p. 58.
8. Psalm 127:3.
9. Mark 9:42, NEB.
10. Acts 2:38, 39, emphasis supplied.

Take Your Love to Town

1. 1 John 3:18, NEB.
2. 1 John 4:12.
3. 1 John 4:20, 21.
4. Leo Buscaglia, *Love* (New York: Ballantine Books, 1972), p. 198.
5. Bob Considine, "Could You Have Loved As Much?" *Guideposts*, March 1959.
6. Romans 5:5.